Philosophical Foundation of Education

Srinibas Bhattacharya

ATLANTIC

PUBLISHERS & DISTRIBUTORS (P) LTD

Published by

ATLANTIC

PUBLISHERS & DISTRIBUTORS (P) LTD

7/22, Ansari Road, Darya Ganj, New Delhi-110002
Phones : +91-11-40775252, 40775214, 23273880, 23275880
Fax : +91-11-23285873
Web : www.atlanticbooks.com
E-mail : orders@atlanticbooks.com

Branch Office: Chennai
Phones : +91-44-48531784, 28291383
E-mail : chennai@atlanticbooks.com

Printed & bound in India by Atlantic Print Services

PREFACE

Education is the preparation for life and living to make it meaningful and purposive. Philosophy provides a foundation to determine the objectives of education. The term, philosophy of education, has, no doubt, a popular use. It has a reference to the general aims and objectives and it involves perspectives related to life and living.

The question of values is inevitable in this context. Education helps toward judgement of values.

Decision making is one of the great goals of philosophy of Education. The nature of right decisions has to be related to both education and philosophy.

For this purpose the personal self has to be discussed in various contcxts.

Philosophical foundation has its special significance because of its bearing on other perspectives of education viz. sociological and psychological.

There are other related issues including freedom and discipline, democracy in education and its application in classroom teaching etc.

Lastly, educational theories have evolved round the modalities of approach of life. Realism, idealism, naturalism, scholasticism and pragmatism have influenced educational theories at different ages, no doubt. They are known as schools of philosophy, with their implications.

Thus, philosophy of education is a comprehensive area of knowledge with an interdisciplinary approach.

SRINIBAS BHATTACHARYA

CONTENTS

PART I

PHILOSOPHICAL FOUNDATION OF EDUCATION

1

INTRODUCTION

PHILOSOPHY AND EDUCATION

Significance of education cannot be fully appreciated unless it is looked at in proper perspectives.

Education has more than one perspective, viz., philosophical, sociological and psychological. A comprehensive view of education leads to a sound philosophy of education.

In the field of social science there is a considerable overlap between one aspect and the other. Yet, they have something in common. All these disciplines are related to men. Thus education as a subject for study draws its materials from different areas including Psychology Philosophy, Sociology, etc.

The philosophical perspectives provide the basis of education in terms of values, aims and objectives. Education as a subject should have a value-orientation for its impact on philosophy society and other factors of education.

The interaction between these areas has made the interdisciplinary approach feasible today.

The philosophical basis of education seeks to support the need for a direction which education should follow. It provides directives and offers values to which education should be oriented from time to time. It is assumed that the knowledge of metaphysics and ethical thinking helps an educationist to put education in the proper perspective.

The philosophical basis makes education more purposive towards ends which are fundamentally good. Thus education without philosophical basis remains rather shaky.

In the words of Reid, "If education is a purposive activity of the utmost importance for the welfare and growth of young human beings, the most careful critical and constructive thought about ultimate purpose of education is surely necessary''

Values are different and the bases of education, society and social perspectives are hard to ignore. The social environment determines, no doubt, the needs and problems to be met by means of education.

The principles of sociology when applied to education create the required perspective for its effective operation in the context of social interaction in a community. School is considered as a community where students, teachers and administrators are like community members. Teachers function like parents and heads are like leaders in the community. The students socialize while learning and playing with their peer groups.

Social control is exercised within the school when socialization takes place.

The various forms of interaction within and outside groups determine the quality of learning experience.

Education is life itself. It is dynamic. It involves the process of interaction. It is also viewed as an experience which is gathered in our life time.

As education is life, so life also is education. We learn by living and live by learning. Living and learning go together. Education has more than one dimension. In a formal sense education comes through learning but in general it involves experience, stimulation and growth. Formal education is only one way of promoting the growth, enriching experience and developing attitude. Thus various domains of human life are touched by means of education. In other words, thinking, feeling and acting are enriched by means of educational experience.

It is obvious to have a philosophical foundation of Education. Without a philosophical basis education tends to lose its direction. Philosophy provides the values, goals and wisdom. In fact, if we are to educate, we must do it with a sense of direction. Priority of values should also be determined for being instilled in the mind of the learners. As philosophy is the key to love and wisdom, it is a necessity in life and education. Our life demands not only knowledge but also wisdom. Without it education is of no avail. From the dawn of civilisation man has been marching in search of wisdom and he is still doing so. In fact, this eternal search goes on. Various experiments are projected through education, so that humanity, happiness and harmony be wedded together.

As mentioned before, education has more than one perspective. It appears that philosophy is the starting point of human progress. It is like a beacon star in the darkness of ignorance. Man finds his way with the help of philosophy which shows the path of life shrouded in mystery. Without the philosophical foundation, therefore, education will be like a boat without a rudder. No doubt, metaphysics is the origin of philosophy. It is not everything in education. Philosophy of education is however limited in its approach as there are other perspectives of education. Exploration and experimentation are the twin methods of unveiling the mystery of life. It is imperative that there should be a direction and destination for whatever we want to do. Thus philosophy of education in general is important as it is the application of philosophy in the field of education. On the whole we attempt to educate for helping individuals to reach perfection. To attempt to educate is to do something intentional and purposive towards what is believed and to be good.

EDUCATION AND PHILOSOPHY

Aims of education come under the purview of philosophical foundation of education because one should know the ends and not the means alone. Education comes from the Latin word "Educare" that is to bring up to foster, to lead. It is, therefore, necessary to set some objectives to be reached through education. Whitehead says, "The only object of education is the development of complete life". Thus it involves a continuous process of socialisation for adjustment to reality. In other words, education consists in the manipulation of experiences and the potential of an individual towards better adjustment to life. In fact, education and life are inseparable.

A persisting controversy over the priority of values has disturbed the desired balance in educational planning. The various schools of education are emerging in a complex world-society today. Education was bipolar, but today it has become multipolar. This has added to the complexity of the problem confronting the planners in education. There are so many considerations like mind, matter, individual, society, community, group, nation and universe. It is not an easy task to come up with a perfect framework of education which meets all the challenges presented by the different frontiers of life.

FUNCTION OF PHILOSOPHY

The speculative function of educational philosophy is, therefore, closely related to its function of determining the values which education ought to pursue. Taken together, these aspects of educational philosophy would seem to indicate that it has a prospective reference and that it anticipates and directs practice. While there are many who agree that philosophy should provide certain ideas at which teachers should aim, there are others who take a less ambitious view of educational philosophy. Philosophy is retrospective rather than prospective in character. It is more of conservation than progression. The place of Dewey's concept of democracy in education and pragmatism in education deserves special mention. Most readers would admit of its profound limitations when applied to education. We run into problems when philosophy has to decide what is feasible. It is not proper for philosophy to decide what to do in any particular case as it deals with knowledge and not with opinions.

Two types of educational philosophy seem to be emerging. One stresses a dynamic nature, rich with novelty and varied individualities. It does not overlook the need for stability but it also refers to the social culture which is constantly subject to revision in the light of future events. The other approach to educational philosophy gives full recognition to dynamic world. It also points out the stable factors of culture and the primordial traits of reality. It would be proper to keep both these perspectives in view.

The function of education is not only to help the individual to adjust to his environment but also to contribute to the social and cultural environment. In other words, education helps one's adjustment to environment either by passive acquiscence or by active interaction with it. If we go back to the fundamental issue as to whether education should have a philosophy or not, we find a difference of opinion. As mentioned earlier, there are many who hold the view that education is a dynamic process and should have no definite and permanent goal. In that case philosophy of education will have limited significance. Of course, education should have some fundamental and basic aims. Otherwise it will be completely at the mercy of time agent. According to Bertrand Russell, education should have an autonomous existence. It should be effective when it evolves some process for meeting the fundamental needs of society.

As suggested by some educationist like Dewey education should be one of the most dynamic forces. He objects to any static and fixed goal being set as he believes in pragmatism and progress. We should be aware of means to the end and the end as well. Dewey's philosophy of education strongly believes in creative functions of school. Perfection for him is not easy to reach as it involves a continuous pursuit.

Another aim of education is to pass on the social heritage which is the result of the stored experience. While transmitting the heritage the school can either be conservative or be progressive. It is also the function of education to provide knowledge of the various perspectives. In short, philosophy helps to develop a comprehensive outlook. It is through philosophy alone that one's approach to life proves effective. The modern philosophy in education involves a rational outlook which takes into consideration the entire spectrum of life before conclusion. In other words, education without philosophy is incomplete as they are mutually interdependent.

PHILOSOPHY AND EDUCATIONAL ASSUMPTIONS

As mentioned earlier, education is a purposive activity towards the following ends which are deemed to be good:

(a) Acquisition of skills.

(b) Passing on of the cultures and traditions of society.

(c) The development of critical minds.

(d) The development of character and personality along the right line.

Philosophy applied to education helps the educationist to put his thought and work into proper perspective. The philosophical assumptions with implications about four different things are around:

(a) Belief about Values.

(b) Belief about Religions.

(c) Non-religious Metaphysical Belief.

(d) Belief about Knowing.

(a) *Belief about Values.* The four kinds of assumptions affect education. They overlap with one another. Beliefs about values are important in educational thought and practice.

All the factors of education are influenced by the values. The aims and objectives, the content of the curriculum, the teachers' outlook, the methods of teaching and evaluation are all influenced by belief about values. There are certain educational values which appear to be more desirable than the others. Love for the children and love for knowledge are the most desirable attributes of a good teacher. Similarly a deeper understanding of human nature and education enriches the professional growth of a teacher.

(b) *Belief about Religions.* Belief about religion leads to belief about values. Humanism which is characterised by concern for human beings is a matter of prime concern almost in every religion. There is difference between kinds of humanism leading to differences about religion, but the importance of human being is acknowledged by every one.

A humanist believes in the well-being and the happiness of human beings. Nevertheless there are differences between kinds of humanism leading to difference around religion. It is easy to misunderstand the distinction between the types of humanism. The beliefs about religion are the determining factors which form the basis of classification of humanism. This belief helps the teacher to develop his own philosophy as a guiding force in his personal and professional life.

(c) *Non-religious Metaphysical Belief.* There are many forms of metaphysics in which religion is not directly involved. This has a bearing on educational assumptions. In psychological studies we usually make our objective approach without any reference to religious or metaphysical belief.

(d) *Belief about Knowing.* It is not belief but facts which guide our assumptions. Particularly behaviourism depends more on facts and objective data. Moreover, it assumed that education is conditioning. From this point of view a child is to be moulded and shaped according to the expectation of the society.

2

PHILOSOPHICAL FOUNDATION OF EDUCATION

NATURE, SCOPE AND FUNCTION OF PHILOSOPHY

The traditional concept of philosophy has been developed for ages with reference to metaphysics. It deals with the knowledge of the universe, the ultimate reality and its source or origin. Thus philosophy directs its enquiry into life in its totality. It also deals with the aim and purpose as well as some other relevant issues and problems around life. The task of philosophy is also to unfold the mystery behind creation and the creator. No doubt, it draws its data with the help of introspection, logical analysis and observation. It is still considered as a discipline based on metaphysical statements and propositions.

Philosophy is a term which is based on the concept of life and knowledge. It is an attempt to understand the world of experience in different perspective. "The nature and function of philosophy is itself a kind of philosophical problem over which there have always been controversies," says Reid. Philosophy is love of wisdom needed most in our life. A philosopher is the lover of wisdom who can see life steadily as a whole. Inspite of the differences of opinion about what is philosophy, there is an overall agreement on the meaning of philosophy. O' Conner believes, that it is a mistake to assume that philosophy is a sort of superior and profounder science. Metaphysics has emerged as a separate branch of knowledge to explain life and its purpose. Besides, it deals with certain issues around truth, knowledge and wisdom. Since time immemorial the mysteries of life and death are presenting challenge to mankind. It is only the philosopher who approaches this issue with a total outlook. Plato and Socrates have tried to deal with the question of life and living, reality and appearance and have thrown new light on these areas. Philosophy helps man to attain a clear and consistent conception of world system. The universe is the whole and its origin, function, destiny and end are the factors of the world system.

The scope and function of philosophy are no doubt, limited. The primary responsibility is to understand the nature of reality in all its dimensions. All the sciences started as branches of philosophy in a very general sense to cover all enquiries. In the past, philosophy was regarded as a specialised discipline relevant to education. This approach has been modified in recent years. Today philosophy is assuming a more operational magnitude. As a discipline it has enriched a number of areas of knowledge by providing a stronger foundation than any other branch of knowledge.

It offers a comprehensive outlook to serve as a link between the various isolated disciplines.

The moral and spiritual values and the relevant problems have been the topics for discussion in the area of philosophy. The basic assumption is that people must live in happiness with a purpose. With a view to ensuring this the following must be considered:

(a) The existence of the individual and individualism.

(b) Understanding the need for love, kindness and acceptance.

(c) Cultivation of capabilities and right frame of attitude.

Thus philosophy has also the following roles to enrich human life:

(d) Creating a self concept.

(e) Learning certain human relations.

(f) Inclusion of positive attitudes, human dignity, etc.

(g) Learning of cultural sets.

Besides, the philosophers have undertaken the challenging task of generating values.

It goes without saying that approaches to the study of education demonstrated the need for philosophy as a conceptual frame-work. Thus educational philosophy emerged as a concept for dealing with the philosophical issues and problems in educational perspectives. It is, however, viewed as speculative branch of study which attempts to get an overview of the entire field and putting various parts together into a system. It is no wonder that some describe the function of philosophy as synthetic rather than speculative.

Education is the core of almost all the social sciences. This is a purposive activity, a process and not a product. One can ask if education should have some ultimate objectives. This is a controversial issue and one fails to give a straight answer to this question. The basic query is whether education should have a philosophy. It does not mean that it should be bound by some set of values. Philosophy provides a vision and a wide perspective. One might ask if education can be thought as an independent autonomous function without any reference to any set of goals. To Dewey, education is life itself, and it is as dynamic as living. As we live, we learn and educate ourselves. This is a pragmatic view of Dewey. In fact, we need some frame of reference in which education has to fit into. No doubt, various schools of philosophy have emerged with their distinct bearing on education. It appears that education should be consistent with certain fundamental values in life. There exist truth, goodness and beauty as criteria. The question arises whether these dimensions of life, can be reached through education. It is obvious that goodness and truth cannot be divorced from beauty and happiness. Education for happiness is the ultimate concern of all.

Plato provides us with the psychology of education. Education is not mere acquisition of knowledge, it is the formation of mind. Knowledge can not be imposed from outside. Education is concerned with life. Athletic exercises and intellectual pursuits are all needed for the development of body and mind.

Plato does not forget that life has more than single purpose which a man may consciously pursue. As there are in man reason, spirit and desire, each of these must be developed by training and education. Through experience and education a human being grows towards maturity. Life becomes a perpetual striving for the fulfilment of his physical or spiritual need. To be able to fulfil this need adequately one must clearly understand what the need implies. The impulse must not be blind. It should be directed properly through education. There has been always a controversy over definition of philosophy. Yet, one should have a philosophy of life behind day to day functioning in this age of confusion. Life in order to have meaning and direction should be guided by philosophy.

Philosophy as a vision helps us to look at life and creation in wider perspectives. Metaphysics in the opinion of Ewing, helps one to make genuine discoveries of truth.

In short, philosophy of Education is the application of philosophy and its methods in the field of education. Education is a purposive activity towards the objectives determined primarily by philosophy.

It is a process of enabling one not merely to live but to live adequately. There are various aspects of education, academic, aesthetic, moral, physical, social and spiritual. Theories of education have been formulated and different values emphasised. It is not very difficult to trace the evolution of educational theories. Monasticism has laid emphasis on the orthodox moral values, while the importance of knowledge and learning has been emphasised by the scholastic school. No body cared for the child or the education until the school of naturalism made its bold appearance. Rousseau is the pioneer of this school and it was he who laid the foundation stone of "New Education" or 'paedo-centric' Education.

The horizon of education is gradually expanding. New education is tending to be psychological and at the same time sociological. The human values in education are gradually gaining recognition. The role of education has changed to a considerable extent because of a persistent human effort towards better adjustment of life. The modern movement in education is concerned with the child and its development in relation to his life and environment. It has embraced everything that comes on the way to the development of child. It has regarded humanity as the final object of its concern, and the human mind as a sole creative source. Man is the measure of everything according to the new school. There is some amount of idealism underlying the philosophy of new education. On the one hand there is man with all his potential needs while, on the other, there is total environment. Education has the function to aid in the growth of human potential in all its aspects. The entire outlook has undergone change because of the advent of new education. Every one has welcome it because of its close relationship to life. Today education can also be thought in terms of happiness and harmony. The concept of freedom has been wedded to that of discipline in the area of new education. Education for world citizenship has been considered important today. Democracy in education has been accepted as a mode of living. Both ethics and materialism have been combined and a compromise arrived at before the ultimate goal was pronounced by Dewey. Experience, according to new education, is a precious thing in life which cannot be separated from our existence. Our life is a treasure house where experience is precious. It is through our experience we feel and grow. New education believes passionately in the value of experience and spontaneous expression of the self. Dewey has no doubt, badly come forward with his new and progressive education. Yet the concept of education is shrouded in mystery because of the lack of precision in defining the purpose of education. The goal and direction of life are, of course, determined by human beliefs and needs. Some of these depend on judgements of values.

Today education has become experimental as a science in the laboratory of human life. The old notions and values are changing giving rise to new sets of belief and human values determining the nature of education. His environment expands or contracts as life and learning continue.

Society provides a social environment and education should help one to adjust to it. Kilpatrick and Russel have regarded education both as a force in life as well as a social control.

THE BEARING OF PHILOSOPHY ON EDUCATION

Philosophy, therefore, means looking at a question in its entire perspective. It demands self-consistency and comprehensive outlook. A philosophy of education, therefore, should take into account the conflicting values and notions of life and education. It deals with life, values and religion though it need not be associated with any particular creed.

NEED FOR PHILOSOPHY IN EDUCATION

In order to bring out one of the important points of contact between philosophy and education the issue of value and value judgements should obviously be discussed. In fact, philosophy provides a framework within which education and educational problems can be discussed. Education without any reference to philosophy loses its goal as the aims of education are mainly determined against the criteria set by philosophy. Besides, the philosophical perspectives help the teachers and educators to set the broad as well as specific objectives of education with reference to socio-cultural contexts. The philosophical basis of education is a must for any social science like education because of its dependence on the value of life and society. Of course there lies a controversy as to the role of philosophy in education. According to a particular school, education should be free from any dictation of philosophy and values. Particularly pragmatism advocates this approach with a view to building up the science of education on an independent basis. No doubt, there are certain questions of philosophy which have a direct bearing on educational theories. Any synthetic approach encouraging the combination of values and judgements is possible if philosophy is kept at the centre as a focal point. Possibly one might raise more fundamental question as to whether education is preparation for this life. By education, however, one means adjustment to the environment to bring a desirable change in habits, behaviour, thought and attitude. While philosophy tries to harmonize the different approaches towards life, the function of education is to help the pupils to adjust to the environment.

It is often remarked that every teacher should have a philosophy. A philosophy of education is often adequate to make immediate resolutions to conflict. As a matter of fact, the philosophical outlook has to develop in order to make education harmonious and self-sufficient. The philosophic method which is different from the scientific one, is not directed towards a solution of just a limited number of factors or variables to be controlled experimentally. A philosophical study of a problem may become very complex. Thus the data which educational philosophy draws into synthesis are often derived from a wide variety of sources. Indeed, religion which is closely akin to the philosophical enterprise is also interested in exposing the educational problems.

ONE OR MANY PHILOSOPHIES OF EDUCATION

While it is generally agreed that the unity of outlook is the legitimate objective of educational philosophy, the manifold details with which it deals may not reduce to a single principle of interpretation. There are some philosophies which succeeded in achieving a unitary point of view or synthesis. But other philosophies find unity in diversity The educational philosophy of democracy has to promote the cultivation of diverse personality or cultures. Without any definite philosophy no educational structure can help the cultural development. Philosophy has got other responsibilities as well. In spite of the existence of a few schools of educational philosophy, the claims of educational philosophy to be grounded on an ultimate reality may lead to one single philosophy in education.

THE CONTENT OF EDUCATIONAL PHILOSOPHY

The difficulty we find in drawing a line of demarcation between the proper spheres of philosophy and science in education is not to be overlooked. Originally an advanced study of philosophy is based on common knowledge and gives rise to differences as well. As various sciences have evolved, a tendency towards specialization has been observed leading to the important subdivisions of educational philosophy. A controversy arises as to whether philosophy is at the root of education. There are three aspects which are principally concerned with education. They are: (a) theory of values, (b) the theory of knowledge and metaphysics, and (c) the general theory of reality. In examining the aims of education, the motivation of learning and the measurements of its results, are relevant. We are to deal with ethical problems and problems of value as well. Values are also important considerations in selecting the appropriate curriculum. The curriculum being the avenue for approach to knowledge helps us to understand the nature of knowledge. The nature of knowledge will not only influence the way in which the curriculum is organised, it will also help toward formation of the concept of truth. One will have to consider the nature of human elements as well as the world from which such problems emanate. Both will constitute the content of educational philosophy. Educational philosophers hesitate to admit of the importance of metaphysics. As such the need for metaphysics can hardly be overemphasized. A progressive education, therefore, admits of value of educational philosophy as a dynamic concept. They do not feel like accepting educational aim as fixed or final. They define education as the continuous reconstruction of experience.

Critics and opponents of progressive education can find themselves confronted with different issues of world. While recognizing the consistent world they reflect that there is much in the world that does not change. Thus greater significance to the enduring and changeless set up is emphasised. Consequently education is considered to have some definite pattern and goals which it seeks to realize.

3

INDIAN PHILOSOPHY OF EDUCATION

Introduction

Before formulating the principles and philosophy of education we should remember the following facts:

1. India is a country of villages with diversity.
2. India is a country of many languages.
3. India is a land of many religions and values.
4. India is a land of many prophets and spiritual leaders.
5. India has emerged as an important country or nation in the Third World and is also an advocate of peace and harmony.
6. India needs democratic principles in socio-political and educational life. She enjoys the largest democracy.
7. She has the progressive outlook and her desires to develop science and technology should be projected in every sphere.

All the above considerations should be projected while developing the philosophy of Education in India.

The curriculum and the co-curricular programme should be developed with a view to reaching the objectives set for Indian education.

The programme of evaluation should also be developed according to the objectives of education.

Evolving an Indian philosophy of education demands a study of Vivekananda, Tagore, Gandhi and Sri Aurobindo, with their relevance in modern India.

With a view to evolving an Indian philosophy of education, we need to understand the basic values guiding the life and education of Indian people. A close study of the history of education in India leads to the observation that different values have emerged at different times in Indian history. Yet one can hardly ignore the fact that Indian education remained insensitive to the needs and demands of the Indian society.

At times idealism appeared to influence education in ancient India while naturalism proved dominant in determining the educational environment for the total development of children's personality.

Traditional Indian education is naturalistic among adivasis and tribal people of India but the Western form of education prevailed among young Indians who were exploited by the British rulers and used as clerks or assistants. This system of education was far from being perfect.

Since India won Independence, attempt has been made to formulate a national educational policy. Various Education Commissions have been set up for reorganizing the educational system including the syllabus, examination system and method of teaching.

It has been considered essential to evolve an Indian philosophy of education in the light of the tradition and culture upheld by Vivekananda, Tagore, Gandhi, Sri Aurobindo and others.

India is known for her diversity in values and lifestyle. One has, therefore, to take into account all these Indian values and needs to finalize the blueprint of Indian education. A review of the socio-political trends in modern India shows mixture of various creeds and needs posed from time to time.

She has also imbibed a few western values. A new education has emerged as a result of this blend of cultures and values.

Democracy has finally taken root in Indian way of life. India in a world context presents the problem of reconciliation between various forces. The Western socio-cultural values may be in conflict with those of India. Yet India has absorbed some of the principles including democracy and pragmatism.

Idealism is replaced by pragmatism with the passage of time and democracy by the socialistic pattern of life.

In view of the currents and cross-currents in Indian society, an attempt to approach toward Indian philosophy of education should be made.

In fact, the needs and problems of India with reference to its aspirations have to be projected in the national policy of education today.

Every nation needs an educational philosophy for building up a sound system of education. India has passed through various stages of development during different periods. Since Brahmanic-education it has followed the monastic, scholastic, realistic, idealistic and pragmatic trends when values changed and new priorities emerged.

Recent development in Indian history have shown the need for setting up various Education Commissions to cope with the challenge of time. Yet we find loopholes and limitations in our educational system.

It is unfortunate that in spite of various experiments conducted in India at different stages after Independence, we find the problems of unemployment, youth unrest and national disintegration. All this shows disharmony and imbalance between the community needs and expectations as well as educational outcomes.

This is why a sound Indian philosophy of education needs to be developed, before long.

Criteria for determining the priorities of goals have to be set for planning and development of Indian education. Some important issues are:

(a) National integration

(b) International understanding

(c) Community and social awareness

(d) Indian economic goal and strategy and

(e) Cultural goals and values.

It goes without saying that mere idealism and scholasticism are not enough.

Conclusion

India is a land where values have emerged and influenced the cultural life of the land. It is observed that she was absorbed various religions and philosophies. Yet she has retained a unique style by blending naturalism, spiritualism and humanism.

With the changing time and socio-political trends objectives of education have changed. The ancient system of Indian education has a priority on spiritual aspect of human development while the modern science and technology with its impact on lifestyle and values have brought about a significant change in the area of educational philosophy.

The cross-cultural studies of modern values show an increasing tendency toward materialistic and self-centred outlook.

The world in which we live today is shrinking everyday, but every nation is busy in building, a wall of prejudice.

This is why we need to develop an Indian philosophy of education. The history of education shows how the different rulers have tried to use education for their political purposes.

In fact, Independent India badly needed a separate philosophy of life and education with emphasis on her cultural and traditional traits.

DEVELOPING AN INDIAN PHILOSOPHY OF EDUCATION

To start with we have to discuss what is typical of Indian philosophy. It is the history of Indian philosophy which will tell the stories of philosophers with their different propositions. As already known, India has passed through centuries which have witnessed the changes of outlook and faith. Right from the ancient ages of Brahmanic education we find different emphasis in terms of values and priorities. It is likely that the spiritual quest has become a fashion at certain age, whereas the thirst for knowledge dominated in the area of education for a while. Thus the monastic and the scholastic schools emerged one after another presenting the modalities of values for projection in the field of education. While these two schools dominated over Indian philosophy, the other schools developed as realism and idealism. Of course, realism could never be a school by itself as this emerged as a reaction to life. In fact, realism is an attitude rather than a school. Unfortunately there is a lot of confusion about the term reality. Reality, in fact, is a phase of life which is based on our experience and sensation. This is why the same reality appears to be different to different people. Subjectivity creeps in as a reality is perceived from different angles. In short, reality does not ignore the needs and demands of either individual or society.

As mentioned earlier, the need for building up a rational philosophy of education is imperative. This should be done in terms of values and goals for being reached through education. It goes without saying that India is known for her spiritual and idealistic outlook. It will be, therefore, quite usual to emphasize values in certain direction. Certain values are to be generated for using education as an agent for social change.

No matter what values or value promoters are selected for Indian philosophy of education, we can hardly forget that the world today is shrinking fast. This is why a fusion of values is bound to occur. On the one hand, we should look back for searching the permanent human values from tradition and culture of the country, while on the other we should look forward to future possibilities. Thus attempt should be made to retrospect and introspect for the prospect of a sound philosophy of education in new India.

ANCIENT SYSTEMS OF EDUCATION AND THEIR BEARING ON PHILOSOPHY

Buddhist Education

While the Brahmanic education was mainly based on Vedic concepts, the Buddhist education was more accommodating and open. It was the result of strong reaction against the rigidity and narrowness of the Brahmanic system. The door of the Buddhist monasteries was wide open for all castes and the austerity, laid down by the Brahmanic system was discouraged. The conditions for admission to the 'sangha' for receiving Buddhistic education were very simple. In fact, the main requirements for one's admission were that he must be free from certain diseases and he should neither be a slave nor a debter. The ceremony for the admission was called the 'upasampada' and no one could receive the 'pabbajja' ordination till he was eight years of age. There were strict rules as to chastity, poverty and abstinence from worldly pleasures. Respect for superiors was required from the 'novice'. Each 'novice' (samanera) was required to choose a 'bhikkhu' who was a full member of the order as his preceptor. As mentioned earlier, the pupil was bound by certain rules of conduct toward his preceptor who, on the other hand, had his responsibility towards the pupil. Among the centres of learning 'Nalanda' deserves special mention. Various courses of study were prescribed at different levels and they included grammar, arts, medicine, logic, philosophy and lexicography. In addition to these, certain special advanced course was also prescribed for advanced students. They included the 'Mahabbhasya' of Patanjali, the 'Bhartrihari Sutra' and the 'Bharatiya Sastra' as well. Grammatical study of the Sanskrit language was indispensable. Every student, from the age of six, had to study grammar until he was twenty. In fact, the value of Sanskrit grammar was recognised for the development of mental discipline. Emphasis was laid on discussion and debate, and not merely on lectures.

Although Buddhism encouraged a life of separation from the mundane world of desires, it did not advocate complete renunciation of the world. Unlike Brahmanic education, Buddhist education imparted some secular knowledge. It was broad-based and more humanistic in its approach.

The relation between the teacher and the student was close and cordial. Sometime the pupils learnt directly as a result of closer contact with the individual life of the 'guru'. Both the pupil and the teacher used to sail in the same boat in the ocean of knowledge. Thus the interaction between the pupils and the guru was more effective and less formal.

Regarding the school environment everything was so simple as much depended upon the spirit of co-operation and understanding underlying the Buddhist education. Lessons were usually repeated aloud and were recited in a singing tone. The alphabet was first learnt and was copied upon 'tal' leaves and the pupil began to write upon sand at times. There was no fixed building for most of the Buddhist schools which are usually held under some shade.

It seems that apart from the monasteries Buddhism did not provide any educational environment. Yet Buddhist education influenced the general mass of the people by providing opportunities for popular instruction. At one stage of the Buddhist religion the monasteries started undertaking instruction of popular nature. Gradually, however, the system underwent some change and an attempt was made to liberalise education in the light of fundamental human needs. No doubt, Buddhism has passed away from India, but it has left behind a tangible influence on Indian philosophic thought and religious ideas. Its curriculum, although meagre, became enriched from the borrowed materials and adopted from the Brahmanic school. The Vedas were replaced by its own sacred books. Thus the Buddhist educational ideals and practice were derived from those of Brahmanism.

Thus, the history of Buddhism traces back to sixth and seventh centuries before Christ. Although this was an extension of Hinduism. It has offered a new approach to life. The Buddhism as a lifestyle has its uniqueness as it attempts at salvation (Nirvana) through three types of Monastery.

On the other hand, the principal aim of the Upanishadic education is, therefore, to educate the mind instead of catering information. According to the Upanishad, education is a process of controlling the mind through self-realisation. Thus yoga has the same purpose of disciplining the mind for concentration.

Even the *Bhagvat Gita* offers much to mankind by way of guidance. It expounds the harmony between the diverse approaches to reality through knowledge, love and detachment. The *Gita* is the most comprehensive treatise with deeper significance for humanity at large. Its educational value is immense and enduring for the entire mankind. Man developed an inner spiritual nature through self-discipline and awareness in relation to reality. It is the question of the integration of our personality and the development of the divine existence which have been dealt both in the Upanishad as well as in the *Gita*. They have upheld the external values of life which should be fostered through education. In other words, the aims of education should be determined against the criteria of perpetual goodness, truth and beauty (Satyam, Shivam and Sundaram).

From the Upanishads we get more sidelights on the ancient Brahmanic education, where preparation for life was emphasised. Even serving the teacher and collecting fruits for him were considered as a part of education. Thus the Brahmanic education was more oriented to basic needs of life. The system also provided a broad basis for the growth of personality. It was both formal and informal as the pupils received verbal instructions at times in addition to directives for self-development through co-curricular activities. No matter whatever the structure of Brahmanic education was, the final objective of self-realisation, dominated over other goals. To establish the harmony between the inner self and the entire creation was another major aim of Brahmanic education. It was through the interaction between the disciple and the teacher that the process of education was completed. The teacher in the Brahmanic system occupied a civilized position of unquestionable integrity. His wisdom and learning were transmitted in course of this interaction and the disciple not only gathered knowledge of the subject-matter, he could make real advance in his spiritual life as well.

The pupil was under certain obligations towards the teacher. He was to remain with the teacher so long as his course lasted. In the Upanishadic texts there are references to cases where pupils wandered from teacher to teacher to complete a course. Certain menial services had also to be performed for the teacher.

This included fetching of water, collecting fuel and sweeping the place around the fire. Rigid rules were laid for the conduct of pupils and adherence to those was enforced. Regarding the approach to education one can visualise the importance of ritualistic pattern of Brahmanic education. *Sraddha* was considered as the primary means of attaining excellence in knowledge. Next came the importance of Samyama or self-restraint, which was given the top priority. (Sraddhaban labhate Jnanam, tatparah samyatendriyah). Regarding teachinques or methods of learning, the Brahmanic system emphasised the role of humility, of modesty, curiosity and questioning as well as service (pranipatena, pariprasnena, sevaya).

The course content under the Brahmanic educational system remained very flexible as it was designed to meet the needs of individual learners. It included humanities, science, vocational education and practical courses. In short, the curriculum was geared to the purpose of living as well as striking a balance between the conflicting values of life.

Regarding the technique of teaching, the question and answer method was popular although at times dialectical and other instructional approaches were followed. The pupils learnt through recital of Vedic texts, daily exercises and performance of duties as well as from examples set by teachers. Nature also contributed to the development of their aesthetic sense as well as healthy attitude.

The pupils were placed in life situations full of challenges and evaluated according to their ability to cope with those problems. There was no formal examination as the teacher (guru) used to test not only their theoretical knowledge but also the toal personality, skill and applied subject knowledge on day-to-day basis. Thus the teacher's recommendation was considered final before he was declared to have been successful in his academic life. Emphasis was also laid on the pupil's attitude toward learning, life and the superiors including teachers. Reverence for the teacher was the most expected conduct from every pupil. Conformity and obedience, modesty and manners formed the part of his duty and obligation. Thus in the Brahmanic educational system academic growth was not considered in isolation. The system encouraged every pupil to attain an all-round development of his potential in all directions so that he could emerge as a full man in his actual life. Regarding the subjects, there was a wide variety of contents catered to meet the intellectual needs of the learners. In fact, the subject-matter ranged from fine arts to medical science including music, arts, humanities, astronomy and social science.

4

HUMAN FACTORS OF EDUCATION

Education itself involves a number of factors as the ultimate objective is to bring certain desirable interactions. It would be a mistake if one takes a very narrow view of education. The modern concept of education is more concerned with the improvement of the total man in relation to his environment. As such, education as a social control has its responsibility. It is a telic process which brings certain change not only in human beings but also is the other factors like method of teaching, evaluation system, curriculum and total environment. If we analyse, it would not be difficult to see that the human factors are of vital importance in the entire set up while other factors are to fit in or adjust to the needs of the human elements.

The human factors of importance, according to priority, are teachers and parents who are supposed to be mainly responsible for the development of a child.

We could hardly expect to orient the parents for the proper upbringing of the younger generation for various reasons. The most outstanding of them is the want of healthy attitude and lack of consciousness of their respective roles in our changing society. The plan for bringing the teachers and parents together on various occasions might serve some purpose while a consolidated programme is badly needed for the development of a proper outlook among the parents in general. Home, is no doubt, the most important place where a child meets most of his needs and gradually gains self-confidence and security in constant association with the members of the family. The present educational system should, therefore, involve the parents in the programmes organised by the school authorities for the purposes of socialization. The role of the teachers is changing along with the role of the school as a community centre. It is felt that there should exist a very close tie between the child's home and school and the gulf so long maintained between the two should be bridged up by all means. Relationship between people involved in education is very important as much depends upon how human motives work in interaction with the toal group and environment. Today we are recognising everything except the human values resulting in the complete confusion among the students themselves and even teachers. It is rather disappointing that the human factors remain ignored if not neglected and the result is quite far from being satisfactory. The lot of the teachers and the students is still to be improved by provision of incentives, encouragement and recognition. The amount of frustration which the people suffer from proves detrimental to any progress in any direction. One wonders as to how situation would improve unless the human resources receive top priority.

The next important factor in education is the curriculum which is often misinterpreted. It is the totality of the experience which is important in the construction of a curriculum. Very often the rigid notions of subject-matter stand out and tend to build up small compartments. As a result, every subject specialist feels tempted to overemphasise his particular subject of specialisation sacrificing the total perspective. It seems that curriculum has been recently regarded as a very important factor for providing the necessary experiences for the preparation of life. At the same time the capacity of the individuals to assimilate knowledge at each stage should not be lost sight of, as otherwise the pupils would be subjected to the tyranny of the educational administrators. The present falling educational standard in certain areas may be partly because of the disharmony between the needs and capacities of the pupil on the one hand and the demands of the educational administrators on the other.

There is, obviously, a scope for misunderstanding on this point and much depends again upon how the knowledge is catered. It naturally raises a very important issue around another factor of education, viz., techniques of teaching. Quite a lot of materials could be presented to the students if they are done in an interesting and skilful manner.

With the advance in the methodology of teaching, it is emphasised that lectures and instructions should be supplemented by means of discussions and seminars or some other methods involving groups and individuals. Apart from that there is a question which has been so much discussed and that is examination. It is rather delicate to assume that examination is a necessity. If so, what should we evaluate? Is it the information acquired or the innate potentials or the acquired knowledge which we want to measure by means of examination? The answer is not so simple as it appears to be.

It is a fact that the examination system has to be geared to the objectives of education. If the aim of education is to develop healthy attitude towards life and skill for preparation of life, the system of examination has to take care of that as well. In this respect, however, our examination system is taking into account only one objective, viz., the academic growth, critical thinking or originality of approach. There is a tendency among the examiners to test what the pupils do not know instead of what the pupils know and this is basically a wrong approach. Very recently the term examination has been replaced by another term evaluation which takes into account all the sides of development of a person in his sojourn of life. Yet the problem remains unsolved. Lastly the Indian educational system has been passing through a period of a very unstable environmental set up emerging in recent years.

The field of education is thus wide involving a number of factors. Every factor is directed towards the improvement of the pupil's learning behaviour. There are certain factors which may be classified under 'human' and certain others as situational. Under human factors we can include parents, teachers, associates and even the neighbours. Under the other category comes a number of situational factors, like method of teaching, learning situation and classroom atmosphere, evaluation system, etc. The purpose is to orient all these factors to the need for development of the pupils.

The concept of a modern teacher is also changing. The function of a teacher is that of a friend, philosopher and guide.

The discovery of the potentials in each pupil is the most important function of a teacher because he has the task of unfolding those potentialities by gradual stimulation. Another important aspect of the teachers' role is the understanding of the pupils with reference to their needs and problems. The third role of a teacher is his participation in the community life so that the gulf between the school and the society can be bridged.

Teacher in Society and Teacher-Education

Teacher occupies a pivotal place in any social set-up. With the emerging social order the teacher's role has changed. He is no longer concerned with the traditional-teaching as he would be concerned with the education of the total child. It is one of his primary responsibilities to build up a new generation of leaders of iron hands, strong will and deep love for the nation and humanity. The teacher will have to enthuse this younger section of population with a spirit of devotion to serve the country and nation. Our nation looks forward to the selfless service of the younger generation with a view to maintaining its power and prestige. The teacher community would be required to generate that power inherent in the student population. Virtually they should be leaders of the young generation and not merely instructors.

Another important role of the teacher today is to promote the standard of community life in our new India. A spirit of social service should enthuse them to extend their function beyond the walls of the classrooms. They should come down to the villages of India to enlighten the poor and ignorant population with sympathy and determination. In other words, the teacher-community today should get actively involved in adult education and community service. Otherwise, the ignorant mass living in the midst of poverty and darkness would definitely impede the progress of young India. Rural education centres and rural universities should be set up for an effective operation. The band of properly oriented teachers should reinforce their activities in close coordination with the schools and institutions at various levels.

Teacher as Leader

What is urgently needed now is the determined leadership of the teachers of new India in building up a better, stronger and happier India tomorrow. In short, the role of the teachers of today should be quite extensive and varied. Teaching should be mainly an inspiration. With the emerging set up the responsibility of every teacher has assumed a very great significance for building up a strong and self-reliant nation of tomorrow. The teacher as a field worker has a wide area to serve, viz., the class, the community and the nation as a whole.

Builder of Academic Life

It has been held for many centuries that the teacher is the caterer of knowledge and one's primary task lies in building up the academic life of the students under the guidance of each teacher. Catering information has been criticised and suggestions have been made to improve the existing techniques of teaching for the development of the intellectual life in the real sense of the term.

Emphasis has now to be laid on the unfolding of the fundamental potentialities, e.g., critical thinking, reasoning and problem-solving capacity. With a view to doing this effectively the teacher has to be resourceful, well-versed in child-psychology as well as in the specific subjects, and keen to draw out the maximum of each child. It is now considered that collection of information in a field of knowledge does not help much in the actual intellectual development of a child.

Creating New Values

It is strongly felt that besides intellectual development, education has the primary responsibility of bringing about emotional maturity and developing sentiments for good, right and beautiful things and ideas. The place of 'Bodha' or sentiment, according to Tagore should occupy a prominent place in education. It is, therefore, almost imperative that a real educationist or educator should foster this spirit among the young children. The children should be taught to feel for others, to love their own country and people and to respect their superiors. What is lacking today is the emotional maturity, in spite of all academic preparation, even among the adults. This stands on the way to development of a healthy outlook in life.

The teacher's social activities are, therefore, no less important than other activities of academic nature. On the contrary, the social role of the teacher community has assumed greater importance during recent years. Attempt should be made to socialise education if not to humanise it. Problems of various dimensions confront the teachers and educators today and it would be a challenge to face them with self-reliance. The teacher community should restore the self-reliance needed for any reconstruction of our socio-educational structure. There should be a reawakening of the entire teacher community so as to inspire the younger generation utterly confused and bewildered about values of life. Unless the teachers accept this challenge with a spirit of dedication and national service there would remain little hope of any real change for the better. They should assert themselves for regaining their leadership captured by the people of other walks of life.

Teaching an Inspiration

With the emerging new social order the system of education is bound to change. It is, therefore, natural that new objectives of education have been formulated by the recent Education Commission. Secondary education in India is undergoing drastic changes and various problems are emerging. It is very often felt that the paucity of suitable teachers is an outstanding handicap in implementing any change.

The concept of education has also changed and so its role. Along with purely academic goals education has to cope with the changing needs of the growing society. The socio-economic factors as well as the political ideals cannot be totally brushed aside. With a view to meeting the demands of every kind, our nation needs regiment of qualified teachers with adequate potentialities. Unfortunately teaching profession is still not able to attract the promising young men who can inspire the young generation and instil in them desirable attitudes. Teaching is mainly an inspiration. There are needs for the teachers to get themselves inspired before they can inspire others.

There was a time when teachers were believed to be only born and not made. There are still people clinging to the old notion attaching great importance to ths scholarship of the teacher and undermining the value of teacher education. The reasons are not far to seek. This old notion can be changed if the impact of teacher education on the student population at various levels can be proved.

Inadequate Teacher Education

The existing programme of teacher education is inadequate for various reasons. It is peculiar that in spite of so many years' experimentation with teacher training schemes in India, the impact of the scheme is not very significant.

The teacher training scheme has not so far been able to take into account the various needs of our schools and community and the desirable roles of the teachers at various stages. It also fails to offer a solid grounding in the subjects taught in schools. Besides, the knowledge of the method of teaching and the various subjects provided in the training course do not cover the recent trends in education, some of the methods being rigid. The methodology taught hardly equips a teacher to face the complexity of typical classroom situation. They are mostly suitable for ideal classroom situation. The training course does not help much is developing an interest in the profession. Nor does it promote any other social growth essential for a teacher's success in his profession. The course also fails to develop a practical skill among teachers so as to ensure success in community participation. It hardly orients the teacher in the art of living a dedicated life.

Teaching — A Life of Dedication

One can seldom deny the fact that teaching as a profession demands certain amount of dedication and spirit of service. This important aspect of education has to be kept in view while drawing up the total teacher-education programme.

India, since Independence has been passing through a number of odds to be partly tackled by means of education. The young generation of today should assume greater responsibilities in shaping the destiny of their nation. It is rather imperative at present that emphasis should be laid on the development of national consciousness and leadership among teachers to start with.

It is clear that the role of teachers is now varied and extensive. It is no longer confined within the four walls of the classroom. The teacher is, no doubt, a very important member in the society and the leadership is expected to emerge from the teachers.

Our teacher education programme should be adequate for meeting the new challenge. The traditional concept of teacher's training refers only to the needs of the school teachers and not beyond that. It is curious to note that such a notion is still persistent among highly educated people. This outlook is at present out-moded because of the increasingly felt need for development of skill in handling the human materials at any level. No matter whether one is a primary school teacher or a university professor, both are concerned with their pupils at different age levels. There is the question of motivation, intergroup relations and social interaction influencing learning and behaviour. If education is more than parochial learning, if it means real adjustment to life, the question of teacher-education at every stage would not be irrelevant. The knowledge of group-dynamics on the part of the teacher would prove extremely helpful for effecting any desirable change in experience, attitude and behaviour of the pupils.

New Dimensions of Teacher Education

With the heavier demand of society on education, the number of dimensions of 'teacher education' has increased beyond doubt. Teacher education should now cover a wide range of population including the college and university teachers. Besides, teacher-education should be more intensive and purposive. It should attempt at the development of a healthy attitude towards the profession, society and nation. It should inculcate leadership so as to help the teachers to inspire the young generation with new ideals. For example, the teachers should be so oriented through the teacher-education programme as to enable themselves to develop national consciousness among their students. This requires leadership and resourcefulness. Teachers would be required to draw up a plan of activities, a suitable curriculum and provide suitable media of communication through audio-visual materials and examples.

With a view to making the teacher-education programme effective both the nature and duration of the course should undergo drastic change. The course should be so designed as to create leadership in education. The following steps appear to be useful for the purpose:

(a) The curriculum should be totally revised so as to cover a wide range of studies in different subject areas, viz., Indian sociology, social psychology and rudimentary social sciences along with child and educational psychology.

(b) The course should be of two years' duration. The first year should be spent for orientation in the teaching profession. A major part of the teacher-education programmes should concentrate on development of proper attitude, national spirit and study of the national problems with their bearing on education.

(c) The course should be residential and there should be sufficient stimulation for a corporate life among the teacher trainees for opportunities of socialisation.

(d) Co-curricular activities and community work should form the major part of the first year's programme along with fundamental studies of sociology, social sciences, psychology of group dynamics etc.

(e) Such teacher trainees should be encouraged to do some social work during his training period and to continue it on his return to his school.

(f) Internal evaluation should be introduced with a view to attaching more importance to the development of a spirit of social service and at the same time national consciousness.

(g) Credit should be given for skills in arts and crafts, physical activities and leadership.

Need for Emphasis on Application

The whole first year should thus be spent as the formative period of intensive teacher-training in methodology. Every teacher trainee might be required after six months' theoretical orientation in method papers to choose his special field and the school where he would have to work at his own initiative and leadership with the headmaster and teachers like a regular member of the staff. The head of the school and the senior members of the staff will have to be entrusted with the task of assessment and a uniform rating scale may be devised for the purpose.

Emphasis should be laid here on the teacher's power of application of the self in taking initiative for activities, community participation and in his building up the relations with pupils and his associates.

In short, teacher education programme should be geared to national interests instead of being confined to academic or professional interests. Unless the teacher-community is oriented towards social objectives of education, the development of national consciousness among the young generation would be well nigh impossible.

A Controversy

A good deal of controversy still persists regarding the aims of education. There still remains a conflict between the academicians and true educationists. This may be resolved by making a pragmatic approach to our emerging problems through education. As a matter of fact, there should be no controversy today on the wider concept of education and its application to reality. As such, education at any level should come closer and closer to reality and our social and national goal cannot be segregated from our educational objectives. Teacher-education programme was being divorced from reality as no national interest was being served by the rigid system of training as well as evaluation. It is, therefore, high time when the whole scheme should be remodelled on a new plan so as to fit in the present context.

Development of the Personality of the Teacher

It goes without saying that example is better than precept. With a view to setting good example before the students it is imperative that the teachers should have healthy mind, spirit and personality. In reality, however, the younger batch of teachers has hardly any love and dedication to their profession. This is the starting point of all the evils creeping in the teaching world. It means that there is a lot of scope for improvement of the personality of the teacher particularly belonging to younger generation. It is, however, a difficult task to change one's personality consisting of so many complexes. The attitude of the teacher towards the student and the profession is of primary concern and much depends upon the teacher's attitude towards his own life. The disposition may be partly modified by the needs of the profession if the teacher has the keenness to do so. For example, a teacher can be very friendly and can take the position of a real partner in the same field. A smiling face adds to the grace of this profession.

The next important function of a teacher is to command love, respect and confidence. This can be done only by demonstrating the genuineness of interest in the student's welfare and benevolence. The changing time has necessitated to build up a bright image of a teacher different from that in the past. He will have to be more dynamic at the same time.

There are certain common codes of behaviour which every teacher should follow with a view to maintaining a certain standard in his personality manifestation. He should be polite in his expression on the one hand, while his personal interests should be sacrificed for the sake of his professional growth. Optimism along with cheerfulness would help to inspire the children. A teacher should meet their emotional needs and promote a healthy attitude. Thus a teacher should be mainly a source of inspiration and a fountain head for deriving stimulation. It is apparent that much depends upon the teacher's role and participation in classroom and community.

5

VALUE AND VALUE CHANGES

VALUES IN LIFE AND EDUCATION

Life is the expression of the infinite and it involves the process of gradual unfoldment.

Thus life is dynamic and it has a constant flow. As human beings we have to live to love and love to live. Man is the crown of creation and everything centres round his human existence. Humanity is thus the prime concern for education which should be geared to some purpose. One wonders as to what should we live for and how we can attain that. The concept of values is important for answering the question. Various assumptions about values are projected in life and education. These assumptions not only help the moral guidance but also the educational guidance. The criteria for determining the aims and goals of life and education are many. Often we mention about the three fundamental criteria, viz., truth, beauty and goodness. Keats has pointed out that truth is beauty and beauty is truth. It is obvious that without the values our life is like a drifting boat without any anchor. At present the mankind is facing a period of confusion, conflict and confrontation. The reasons are not far to seek. We have lost direction and values in this age of transition. No doubt, values are different and they may change from time to time. Yet the intrinsic values hardly change as they permeate through ages, irrespective of social and political contexts. Happiness is the goal of life and without harmony we cannot get happiness. It is, therefore, necessary to combine these for the well-being of humanity. Lastly one can hardly deny the need for instilling values in our individual and group life for attaining happiness.

There are ways of comparing vlaues but we may synthesize them profitably. In fact, there are three ways of comparing values. The first one is to do that in a normative way. In this sense things are either positive or negative and we have to choose set of values. In other words, values are arranged in dichotomy that is in terms of opposite, i.e., good or bad, high or low and so on.

The next way to compare values is different. Here the comparison is made on a different frame of reference. The concept of contrast is not the same as in the first case. Although one may think that such comparison tends to be arbitrary, it is not exactly so. The distinction is based on a more subjective criterion.

In the third place, comparison of values may take place without any reference to the traditional way of judgement. In fact, different values may emerge on different occasions. Their fulfilment is demanded by human needs in life. In short, values are of different types and they assume various dimensions in different perspectives of life. Preliminary survey of different values shows the relationship between needs and values. There are moral and religious values on the one hand, while social and cultural values are hard to ignore. Besides, there are values which are functional where the traditional approach to life is not followed. Peace, beauty, love, sansitivity are some of the dimensions related to values. No doubt, value beliefs have some bearing on actual values as they determine their nature and type. Very recently the need for teaching values has been felt both in the east as well as in the west. The question remains as to what values should be taught and how. No doubt, there are values and values and much depends upon the social and political need. Yet there are some fundamental values of life which are permanent through the ages, for example, love and compassion for mankind, truth and honesty, sincerity and integrity are the most outstanding values of human beings. In other words, there are certain human values which transcend all other values.

Time has come when we have started looking for these values for revival of our lost civilization. It is unfortunate that we are losing humanity and entrapping ourselves by greed and passion for power and wealth. We plan today sacrificing moral values for material gains. As a result, the identity of man as a rational animal is fading away. People like Bertrand Russell and Sri Aurobindo have shown serious concern for man's survival in the true sense of the term. His struggle through the ages for perfection will be meaningless if it fails to meet the challenge of the modern technological age. Money is the measuring rod of man's dignity and prestige.

It is often heard that the standard of education today is falling. One wonders as to why these standards are gradually declining. There is a strong feeling that education is loosing its impact on the mind of the learners because of the lack of moral values. It is obvious that learning without behaviour is meaningless.

At the secondary level of education teaching moral values is very important as childhood and adolescence are crucial stages of life. The curriculum should, therefore, include contents with moral implications. There should be in literature enough parables, stories and fables with enough moral values. Of course there should be no direct preaching as that defeats the purpose of moral education.

Therefore, the total programme of activities should emphasize the moral tone to promote the character development of the young generation.

It goes without saying that the entire young generation today is suffering from a feeling of insecurity and frustration. They have nothing to hold them, nor have they any inner strength to resist the evil. This is perhaps because of our secular education.

As regards organising the curricular and co-curricular programmes, every attempt should be made to orient the youngsters to the code of living geared to the purpose of spiritual education. It is, however, practical to elaborate the concept of moral education before discussing the methods of imparting them. By moral education we mean education for moral development.

Morality comes from a sense of values which are related to the meaningful life. The fundamental goodness, truth and beauty should be reflected on the canvass of life in such a way that life becomes beautiful, peaceful and harmonious.

Can we teach moral values? It is difficult to teach values in the real sense of the term. It is to be instilled and imbibed. In fact, indirect methods of imparting values should be developed with a view to making them effective. Audio-visual means for generating moral values have to be innovated.

There are few methods of instilling moral values in a formal way. Of them discussion, participation in cultural functions and sensitization deserve special mention. Story telling and listening to the life history of great people, often prove effective. Besides, recital of devotional songs and recitation of poems containing moral values are helpful.

Values particularly moral values are hard to instil because of the complex process of transmission involved. It is experienced that cultural environment enriches decency of outlook and promotes sense of morality.

It is, therefore, imperative that every school should create an atmosphere congenial to the development of moral standards. The ancient texts of wisdom including the Upanishad may be presented in their simple versions along with textual matters. Similarly legends and fables may be narrated very attractively. In other words, the literary values of the texts chosen for moral teaching should be kept in view. Both the curricular and co-curricular programmes should be designed to inculcate the moral values without imposing them on the young minds. The epics of India like the *Ramayana* and the *Mahabharata* have tremendous potential to attract the young minds and inspire the young generation towards goodness and truth. The fundamentals of religion are embedded in these epics and, therefore, they go a long way to the cause of generating transcendental values of life.

The teacher's role in the task of generating moral values is quite significant. They are the friends, philosophers and guides who can stir the minds of the young people, with new ideas, thoughts and philosophy. In fact, their life should be the example and their way of living should be the source of inspiration. It goes without saying that without good teachers, no amount of theoretical education would prove effective. Even the curricular contents may be mixed up with episodes of moral bearing for assimilation by students. Teachers should be resourceful to incorporate relevant materials to suit the interest and ability of the young people according to their needs. Assembly sessions may be characterised by messages from great people and short discourses. Birthday celebration of great people like Buddha, Chaitanaya and Gandhi or Aurobindo may be organised at regular intervals with an eye to the purpose.

Assumption about values are of great significance for education. These assumptions influence not only the curriculum but also direct the other factors in education. Even the aims of education are determined by the values assumed. Education is a part of life and the questions about values in education are of vital importance and are, therefore, inseparable from larger questions of values in life. If we assume that there are values, the question arises whether those should be compared and contrasted. While comparing values in a normative way we generally put positive things such as good and bad. We can also compare in a different way the pairs of values not opposed as good versus bad but as higher or lower. This is nothing but an attempt to have relative values against certain criterion. There is still another possibility of comparing values with one another without judging that some are better or worse, higher or lower than other. It often happens that different values emerge on different occasions presenting different frames of reference. Ultimately it proves difficult to compare the value of one kind with that of other. Yet this question arises in the field of education where different sets of values confront us for necessary selection. If we analyse the values we may classify them under a few headings:

(a) Values agreed by civilised people, as being basic to individual and social development.

(b) Values determined by democratic principles.

(c) Fundamental values of life.

There may be some conflicts of values, yet the aim of education is to strike a balance. The problem lies in determining the weightages of the individual set of values in the total heirarchy around goals of education. In spite of the controversy we can accept some absolute criterion, e.g., happiness and harmony. One of the recent trends is, however, towards pragmatic approach to life. According to this school of thought, education should not have any fixed and any absolute goal. Aims have to be determined in the light of the day-to-day experience and realization of the changing needs of our life and society. There has been certain conflict between individual and social aims of education. But this is nothing but a conflict at the superficial level. Besides, there exists an utter confusion in the mind of the educationist. One wonders if in India education should cling to the old set of values or one should welcome the new concepts of values with an open mind. If we look back we find a tremendous emphasis laid on the development of moral self at the cost of others. Self-realization and even self-deprivation were held in high esteem. But one's functioning is possible in a social context. Thus the individualistic aims like self-development or self-realization are being challenged with the emergence of new outlook in life. Vivekananda described the aim of education as a manifestation of the perfection already in man, while Tagore presented a different philosophy of education. To him education is more an enrichment of the self in respect of feeling. The idealistic concept of education is reflected in a Sanskrit proverb: "Ya Vidya Sa Bimuktaye", that is, the chief aim of education is salvation. Another school of Philosophy takes an extremely realistic point of view of education and emphasizes that education should primarily solve the bread and butter problem.

As the world is getting smaller, one cannot think of living in isolation. It is a pity that we have learnt to fly in air, dive deep into water, but we have not learnt how to live together on earth. This is the problem of all problems confronting us today. For the sake of safety of mankind one has to think how education can ensure peace and progress for better living. It is, therefore, imperative that education should be geared to the ultimate objectives of living with happiness and harmony. If education cannot meet this major aim, man would bring his own doom and destruction by his own misdeeds.

Some Fundamental Questions on Philosophy and their Bearing on Educational Theories

In short, the concept of philosophy has undergone different stages of evolution. Though it popularly refers to love, wisdom and knowledge, it gives rise to a number of fundamental questions. Its purpose is to help one to attain the wisdom of the world or the knowledge of the soul. There are few major concepts of philosophy. Philosophy is a synthesis of all the sciences. It is a universal science which interprets the results of the special science in a consistent manner. But this view suffers from many limitations. The truth of science and the laws of nature discovered by scientists are subject to change and modification from time to time. A comprehensive view of totality is, however, not attained by the scientific method of observation only. Some sort of insight is also needed for philosophy that critically examines the fundamental concepts of space, time, etc. In the opinion of Russell, philosophical knowledge does not differ essentially from scientific knowledge. Thus results obtained by philosophy do not basically differ from those obtained from science.

CHANGING PERSPECTIVES

It is human practice that our society has to motivate good behaviour and set principles to monitor the results of the application of these principles and to reformulate the principles to establish justice. Justice is considered among values as of paramount importance.

Values may be classified as moral values and competence values. Moral values are concerned mostly with the mode of behaviour and not so much with rational values that indicate end-state of existence.

Only certain kinds of instrumental values that have interpersonal focus are indicated by moral values. When violated, the violater suffers from pangs of conscience or feeling of guilt for wrong doing. Competence values are also instrumental values concerned with the aspect of self-actualization. Such values reflect a personal rather than interpersonal focus, and are not that concerned with morality. Any violation in respect of competence value arouses a feeling of shame about personal inadequacy but not so much of feeling of guilt. The difference between moral and competence values gives the feeling of behaving morally on the one hand and behaving logically and intelligently on the other. The latter appearing more competent than former, conflicts are experienced between these two subtle value concepts.

Values though separate as instrumental and terminal are functionally interconnected systems. Values concerning modes of behaviour are instrumental and those are applied towards achieving the values concerning end-state. Guiding ongoing activities is the responsibility of set standards which emerge from values. Conflict resolution and decision-making depend on value systems. Besides motivational functions, value systems have also functions to make life adjustive and defensive, for self-actualization.

Values answer some specific human needs interests attitude, traits, behaviour and social norms. None of these can interpret values in full. All these specific aspects may be in different order, according to their priority of choice, and requirement, for maintenance of style and behavioural adjustment. Each aspect creates a narrow sub-system of value in the larger value system of a person or a group.

Values in the perspectives of philosophy, psychology or sociology cannot be isolated. Philosophy, psychology and sociology are closely interrelated. The predominance of one characteristic develops from its relatedness to the characteristics of the other two.

Philosophical Perspective

A philosopher is bound by space and time and whatever he expounds is subjective. Absolute neutrality or objectivity is impossible. Perceptions of reality determine his values.

According to philosophical perspective we are more concerned with the end-state of existence. We believe that we shall in the long run free from all sorts of fear, stress and strain. This end-state of being is 'Existence-knowledge-Bliss'. To reach this awareness of one's individual identity with the cosmic identity beyond duality is given the highest value by some schools. All modes of actions that help to reach this end-state are considered as instrumental values.

It involves a gradual process to reach this end-state of existences. According to these promises a value hierarchy is formed. This hierarchical value system presents a concept of interrelatedness of existence, between man and all other beings. If value orientation is achieved on the basis of such a concept, individuals and groups can overcome alienation, establish harmony in human relationship. They can also develop ecological balance. This philosophical view of value provides a metaphysical dynamism, generates in human mind a concept of indivisibility. The philosophical definition of value emphasises human preference to move from the state of alienation to the awareness of oneness of individuals.

Philosophically values are concerned with self and related to the constituents of the self, viz., the material self, the social self, and the spiritual self.

Psychological Perspective

Of late our attention has been drawn to the vital importance of values in regulating the affairs of man. We have been made aware by the progress of biological sciences that value formation also depends upon the biological basis. It has always been agreed that social scientists including economists, sociologists and anthropologists are influenced by the value system.

The biological control mechanisms have definite influence on human value formation. This provides us the rationale to accept psychological perspective as a force for value formation. Psychological perspective is caused by uniqueness of cultures, ethnocentricity, theological bias, social inhibitions and tradition. Value orientation can be made a lively affair if the relevant components inherent in these aspects can be identified, scientifically explained and allowed to be retained by people. Further, psychological excitement of depression can be caused by ongoing social events. For preferred value orientation a study of the effects so such events is to be made. A sort of value judgement should be determined, promoted or abandoned, as and when necessary.

The value trusts that democracy, socialism and secularism can create tremendous psychological excitement, and arouse value conflicts

For the purpose of value oriented education special stress is needed to give total exposure to the value contents on these three value terms with uninhibited mind.

Psychological perspective created for our children often leads to value conflicts between various aspects. For value oriented education we need to study in depth all these aspects and prepare a suitable methodology to inculcate the value awareness inherent in all such terms. We should allow our children to make their own decisions on them.

Sociological Perspective

Any study of values and value orientation from sociological perspective demands a thorough evaluation in various contexts with reference to professional, philosophical and human values. These values are not unique to social scientists. The first one is common to all scientists; the second is related to professional practice in all vocations. But the last one may be independent of social perspective. Regarding our study of social perspective greatest stress is needed to see the degree of our commitment of our self-respect (*Sraddha*) for human dignity. Our approach or study may be similar to that we adopt for other values. The three values are basically inseparable but to understand human behaviour on specific perspectives we now need to specially focus on the aspect of recognizing human dignity.

In social perspective perception of truth is related to variables like time, situation, events, relationship commitment and so on. On philosophical basis truth is looked upon as absolute, when truth is discussed as inviolable at psychological level. In societal environment social scientists can accept truth as only a relative value. According to metaphysical perspective truth as a value is eternal and enduring, but in sociological perspective this value takes the form of probability and temporal dimensions.

Professional ethics is concerned with moral values and quality of work-life. An answer to the question whether 'Honesty is the best policy' or 'Honesty is the best principle' will make the position clear. In sociological perspective moral value is relatively higher than competence value.

Value consideration in sociological perspective is related to socio-economic situation, class differences, cultural and religious bias and such other factors.

Man is ever concerned with the ethical concept of human dignity. It is universal to all cultures world over and an enduring one. Historical, political and ethical standards are concerned with the value of human dignity. Values of democracy, socialism and secularism (according to Indian Constitution) provide a unique sociological perspective for value formation. Particularly the value of human dignity related to democratic values is of the highest order compared to the value concept of human dignity conditioned by other than democratic socio politic-economic perspective. In India the sociological perspective provides for a value sense that help to solve the policy problems created by the immense value of human freedom. At the same time the value of socialism as understood by Indian culture, contains irrational ego sense of the value of human dignity and is persuasive to make individuals to behave harmoniously as a component of the society. The value of secularism also is to keep the political power neutral regarding any communal or theocratic pressure but not denying spiritual aspirations through free choice of rituals and beliefs (of course not according to dictionary meaning).

Value awareness of an individual in sociological perspective is conditioned by: on one side by physiology and molecular biology and on the other by society and ecology. The model is: (i) bio-evolution conditioned by values, behaviour and attitudes; (ii) education, religion and socio-economic conditions; (iii) social, economic and political conditioning; and (iv) environmental opportunities and limitations. Deterioration of law and order, large scale unemployment, economic unstability, etc., cause emergence of unconditional values.

Science, Technology and Value

Science and technology are the results of human search of absolute truth and application of its findings for human use. Science is a continuing effort for knowledge of lower degree to higher. Research is central to any effort in the field of science and it is governed by definite rules of intellectual conduct, which allows criticism and invites replacement of methodology. Science works through institutional systems. All these are value oriented actions. So science is never value free. Science cannot make any compromise with values like open mindness, regularity, appropriate choice of alternatives, devaluation of old concepts in the light of new discoveries and so on. To a scientist value of time is a resource which is eternal but never reusable.

Scientific results influence concepts of ethics. Science is not concerned with value judgement but it is the other name of the eternal urge inherent in a man to have knowledge and to know what is absolute; those are the values.

Science also inculcates the value of constraints and teaches us where to stop. It is the result of scientific investigations that can indicate what type of ethics should be given priority for survival of mankind as well as that of preservation and prevention.

Science being a research continuum it includes evaluative and normative issues as values. Values of science are preferred to value contents of superstitions. Too much emphasis on facts is prone to keep a group or community closed, but value search brings in changes, initiates development and sets the model of the liberal democracy.

Technology

Technology can be developed according to need, interest and attitude of people in power in search of increase of wealth in order to establish human welfare or guarantee security. Technological objectives are always dependent on value variables of people who own technological power and decide its application.

Technology brings in social value changes and motivates economic value search.

The instance of the problem of population growth can be taken as an instance of value-technology relationship. Technology has made it possible to isolate pleasure, fertility, and productivity. As soon as it has been possible to arrest fertility, chose the duration between productivity gap, the drive of pleasure value started taking the shape of a newly emerged spirit of freedom. The situation has been reinforced by the technology of medicines. The value of constraint was ignored as inhibition or superstition. But the process did not stop here. New problems and disaster have appeared, search for value of constraint has got restored once again. All these again motivate scientists and technologists to develop new technology.

Because of technological development there has appeared a new perception of nation-state concept due to shift of security value from territorial boundary of a nation-state to a remote defence boundary from the planet earth into the space. In such a situation the emergence of a new value awareness highlights the necessity of an enduring relationship not only of human beings but also of ecological balance.

Application of technology depends much on collective value awareness of mankind.

Science and technology seem to call humanity to build the concept of secularism and look forward towards spiritual concepts as preferred concepts for survival and better living. When we refer science and technology as concepts of values, our view opens up to the grand convergence of metaphysics and physics, the old time appearance of divergence fading out.

Value and Education : Inculcation of Values

Value education will be a total failure if it is considered as teaching of morality exclusively. One need not elaborate the question of inculcation of values; it is an effort to help pupils to develop and open a questioning mind. They are to undertake value judgement strategies concerned with varying situations related to family relationship and obligation, peer-group relationship in classroom and campus life, and neighbourhood situations. Cultural identity and diversity, ethnocentricity, health problems environmental issues, sex life, religions, interculturization, political commitment, and environment come into play. By undertaking exercises in such strategy packages young ones will develop adequate response capability to make appropriate decisions. It is value awareness that can only help decision-making. Educators also can help better with their managerial values in the sphere of education.

Inculcation of values in students is related to a process of learning instead of teaching. In experimental learning and intellectual perception, teachers or parents are the interpretors.

Inculcation of values in the perspective of value and education evidently raises the very important question whether a student entering the process of higher education will have his choice of programme of studies, or institution or faculty related to the values he holds. Whether a student giving high value on being a musician or artist can go for fine arts subjects in the curriculum? Or students placing a high value on humanities will have to choose economics or statistics as his subjects for the value concern of job market? Value priorities of a student may not be ultimate in his choice of a faculty or programme. Other considerations should be allowed as well. Education is a systemic process to help the potential of a student, to attain what he cherishes, to bloom in its fullness. There are, of course, innumerable instances to establish that the value choice of a student is not always based on mature-thinking, still the values he holds will deserve some consideration.

In the context of values and education the reciprocity of value-attitude behaviour is of considerable significance.

1. We must be aware that the value conflicts are more acute among the children and youth of today. They are more confronted by large number of choices than in earlier times. The alternatives presented to them are not only confusing but often extremely bewildering. The hardest job many children face is learning good manners without seeing any. The sophistication of modern society makes it more difficult for them to make the choice because of the complexity of our contemporary life.
2. Parents, guardians, teachers and leaders, because of their limited concern for the younger generation take steps: to impose 'adults' values upon the young, through direct moralizing. They think on the convictions that grow in them through their experiences. Instead of allowing the youngsters to discover their own values, they try to save them from any risk of making their choices of some less preferable values. It is a method of value transfer and not value inculcation. The young generation continuously gets exposures of conflicting values from different forums like schools or colleges, religious organizations, political platforms, diverse intellectual approaches through mass media and so on. They do not fail to discover the dichotomy between theory and practice. They feel hurt and fail to identify the values that will lead them to their cherished goal or motivate them to act in a way that will reflect their dignity and pride or position.
3. Value being a personal concept, there cannot be one single value for all to imbibe. On this logic any indifferent approach in respect of value transmission allows indulgence or even licence. The method fails to bring the desired result.
4. Value transmission is soon to be more effective through the approach of modelling. It is an approach through person to person relationship and the process is dependent on the concurrence between theory and practice in the life of the model.

5. The values-clarification approach gives relatively better result and it can be introduced from the primary stage of school education to the degree level. This approach creates an interest among the participating students, if the approach content is properly related to age groups and made subjectwise relevant to their life situations.

6. Value concepts can be brought in while teaching various subjects. The detailed methodology and pedagogy can be prepared through operational research on value education based on continuing fundamental research on values and our lives.

Teacher Education for Value Inculcation

In the awareness of an urgency for value inculcation, particularly on the perspective of new education policy, it appears that we should apply a two-way approach for programme implementation based on policy decisions. Firstly, steps are to be taken quickly to prepare teacher activists by orienting teachers in groups to a brief course to make them conversant with values and their implications related to behavioural science. The exercise may include the following topics:

(a) Definition of value.

(b) Classification of values.

(c) Identification of the source of values.

(d) To understand the complex nature of value-attitude behaviour.

(e) Value and social norms.

(f) Value changes-technology and other causes including migration and interculturization.

(g) Value religions and *dharma*.

(h) Complication in understanding raised by language difference and linguistic philosophy.

(i) Values and environment.

(j) Values and will-power development for human quality improvement.

(k) Exercises in cultivating will-power.

(l) Values and spirituality.

(m) Training of specialist teachers in graded course: diploma, degree at graduate or higher levels for creating an adequate academic team of personnel for pursuing value-education. Curriculum may be taken as a multi-disciplinary subject to reinforce not only teaching methods in other disciplines but also to achieve a high quality of education environment.

Our work programme needs to include ongoing research on values, value survey slow change of value awareness, environmental perception and relevant aspects related to values. Also continuous evaluation in respect of values through learning-teaching end-results is helpful.

6

AIMS OF EDUCATION

Everything including life has a goal. Life has its function which is related to its aims. Without goal and aims the direction is lost and without direction the functioning is not smooth. Therefore, for effective functioning aim is a must.

Life and education are interwoven in a meaningful way. Dewey considers education as life itself. Every moment of life is pregnant with possibilities. It appears like dew drops and reminds us of its transitoriness. Life is so beautiful because it is transitory. Education provides us with a sense of propriety, priority and perspective. It is also pragmatic as it changes with the ongoing life. A human being comes on earth, grows and lives for a purpose. Education is the process of realising this truth and reaching the goal. The question arises as to what is education and what are its goals. As mentioned earlier, education is both an art as well as a science. It is the art of living and the science of doing. We live to love and love to live with a view to enjoying his creation. The immortal self finds its way through education and culture.

Aims of Education in Ancient India

In ancient India, attainment of self-knowledge was the main goal of education. This spiritual attainment was emphasized in life. In other words, salvation or 'moksa' has been the focus of attention. In the Upanishads, self-knowledge has been acknowledged as the true aim of life and education. To spiritualize education has been the dominant concern in ancient India. Only in the later stages of Indian transition, social aims have been reiterated. Rammohan, Vidyasagar and others considered education as the tool for bringing social change and social reconstruction. In fact, aims of education are determined according to the needs of the society and culture. In ancient Greece, freedom was regarded as the most precious gift of human beings. This is why individuality has received maximum attention in the western countries including Greece. Man has been regarded as the crown of creation and self instead of society has captured the attention of the thinkers of the day. Gradually a shift of emphasis was noticed. Philosopher like Plato tried to seek harmonious development of the individual with an eye to social solidarity. Similarly Aristotle accepted as the goal of education the ideal of harmony between the individual and the society. To them cultivation of goodness, intellect and goodness of character has become the most important goal. Thus in spite of contradictions between individual and social aims of education attempts have been made for a compromise.

The passage of time has brought some changes in the concepts and aims of education, no doubt. But certain fundamental aims remain unchanged. Development of the finer qualities of heart and head has been recommended through the ages. Various schools of Philosophy have emerged. Realism, naturalism, idealism, humanism and pragmation have been propagated by different schools of philosophy.

It is obvious that education in all its perspectives demands certain direction and goal. It is obvious that the basic issue in Education revolves round its relation to life.

Human life needs development and promotion. This is possible if man knows who he is and what he wants. Self-knowledge is thus a vital consideration for happy living. In order to have a harmonious adjustment and functioning man has to discover reality in all its dimensions. The spiritual reality is not to be ignored along with the social, economic and other realities. Man should march in search of wisdom which provides insight into the spiritual world. The mysteries of life have to be unfolded with the help of wisdom and education. Education is thus a means to happy and harmonious living. The philosophical basis of Education looks for the inner values of life and wisdom. It is, however, difficult to define wisdom because of the deeper implication of the term. According to the dictionary definition, "It is experience and knowledge together with the power of applying them critically or practically." Thus wisdom is more important than ordinary knowledge.

As mentioned earlier, value serves as the criteria for determining the goals of Education. Philosophers have raised questions on different values and their importance. There is a lot of curiosity around what is good, what is true and what is beautiful. In fact, truth, goodness and beauty are the key points in life. That is why the poet has rightly expressed "Truth is beauty and beauty is truth". In the ancient texts of Upanishad we hear the echo of the same message, Satyam, Sivam and Sundaram'.

The social perspectives in Education are, however, different in appearance but not in reality. People and their interaction are the main concern of the social life. With a view to realising the goal of harmony in social life we have to adhere to the ultimate reality. One cannot deny that this creation is nothing but the reflection of truth, beauty and goodness blended together. The relation between man and a man, or man and nature is regulated in a spirit of harmony. Education helps in regulating this interaction between different parts of creation. Man as a strange organism has a number of propensities. He is the most unknown creature, still man is the crown of creation. Why? Because he has the mind and ability to build up the edifice of society where a bond of love and understanding strengthens the social fabric. In the world today we find a lot of disturbance in our social life and community. The reasons are not far to seek. The main task of education is to generate a deeper mutual understanding. As a rational animal, man is guided both by his instincts and intelligence. He has frailties as well as nobilities. Unless both these tendencies are regulated and used to serve our social purpose, a chaos is bound to prevail. Unfortunately education today is not helping mankind to attain this balance so essential for harmony and happiness. In the social context we find a lot of confusion about our goals and values. Needless to mention that basically man today is suffering from identity confusion. All kinds of deviant behaviour patterns are the outcome of this confusion leading to conflicts and disintegration.

Bertrand Russell in his book, *Education and Social Order,* has emphasised the role of Education as a tool for social reconstruction. Living together is an art and has to be learnt through experience. Education should be geared to that purpose and priorities are to be laid on the functioning of each individual in harmony with society. Today we have almost forgotten that we are the sons of the immortal (Amritasya Putras). As a result our values are dwindling. Matter today is ruling the mind. Thus we see that our life needs a philosophical approach as we cannot ignore the ultimate and absolute reality. Materialism is a reality, no doubt, but that is not all. It is the part which is gaining priority in modern life. Yet it has no conflict with the totality of experiences. One has to learn how to keep matter under mind and control the greed and passion around matter.

It is a fact that science and technology have made tremendous progress in the modern world. Yet man is suffering from want, poverty and illiteracy. This means that they are lacking in the proper direction. The gross injustice to a section of the people, the exploitation of the poor ignorant people by the rich are creating unrest and disintegration. This has to be handled properly and adequately by means of scientific education. Some believe that with the help of physical and social science the essential goodness of human nature would prevail.

A Critical Evaluation of the Aims in Philosophy

Different aims of education have been recommended from time to time. Yet there is a scope for specifying appropriate directions to be followed by education. It is observed that the educational aims are determined mainly to meet the cultural and socio-economic needs at a particular point of time. There are, of course, some fundamental goals which need to be reached through education. These aims are transcendental in nature as they are independent of the demands of any time or geographical context. Thus the human values provide a broad basis for determining some general aims of education. On a critical study of the trends in education, it appears that there are forces working behind the formulation of educational objectives.

1. Social forces.
2. Political forces.
3. Cultural forces.

The monastic school emphasized the spiritual values while the scholastic aims were more concerned with the academic and intellectual needs. A conflict started between the two schools resulting in an entirely different approach to life.

The philosophic traditions in India are, no doubt, rich and varied. Hinduism, Buddhism, Christianity and Islam as separate religions have contributed to the total Indian heritage. They have, thus, some bearing on education. The main forces working behind the formation of religions and cult may be traced back to the ancient history of mankind. It has been obvious that every religion like every cult or creed has searched for the truth underlying the entire creation. The unfoldment of the mystery has been the function of education. Religion or politics have been employed for satisfying human needs. Education is the major innovation for bringing a change in the outlook and attitude of man for better orientation to reality. It is interesting that certain fundamental values are embedded in almost every school of philosophy or religion. Educational thought is expected to orient itself to the fundamentals of all religions with a view to proving effective.

Culture is mainly sustained by its religious tradition while education deals with total life. The social function comes under the purview of education. In fact, in ancient culture the sacred Indian texts including the Vedas have provided adequate knowledge of the self as well as the Universe. They embody the wisdom and realisation of life beyond formal Education. For example, the Upanishads tend to probe into the area of self-knowledge and man's relation to his creation and creator. The Vedas offer clues to understand the vastness and variety in creation while the Upanishads shift the emphasis from the wonder of the outside universe to the self within. The *Bhagavat Gita* on the other hand, emphasises the joyful fulfilment of one's specific Dharma. Thus the sacred text points out the destiny of man in a different direction.

In order to understand this spirit of Hinduism one has to probe into the basic philosophy and its bearing on the educative process. The perception of life leads to the development of the philosophy of education. It is harmony which is the keynote to creation. In the east, the aim of religion is the realisation of the highest truth. This is possible through cultivation and spiritual discoveries contained in the ancient texts and the scriptures. The aim of education is not only the conservation and transmission of traditional culture but also the need for the renewal of experiences in the personal life. It is the special responsibility of the educator to generate the freedom of spirit.

The Upanishads speak of the highest knowledge called 'paravidya' as distinguished from all other knowledge termed ''Apara-Vidya''. Paravidya is that knowledge through which the ultimate reality is known. The fundamental vision of the unity of all life is acquired with the help of this knowledge. Unity is possible when humility, peacefulness. Self-control and equilibrium are reached as a result of total purification of the mind. It is no doubt important for us to reach the unity of knowledge in order to appreciate the growth of the educational philosophy. In Upanishads education reserved to aid the individual to achieve the extension of the self and its expansion into the absolute. Thus perception of life in the total perspective of the whole has been considered very important as one of the aims of education.

The principal aim of the Upanishadic education is to educate the mind as the creative self in man. It seeks to train the mind through the medium of knowledge rather than to fill the mind only with information.

The supreme knowledge cannot be gained by mere speculation. Realization is important for self growth.

The mission of the Upanishads is the recognition of dignity and freedom of the human spirit.

Realism and naturalism emerged as two distinctive schools in the hope that one would be able to live more adequately in harmony with nature and reality. Yet something is found to be missing in these two approaches. Idealism sprang from a growing dissatisfaction with the existing schools. There was still a felt need for permanent values in education. Idealism encouraged those seeking a spiritual shelter in the midst of currents and cross-currents of new ideas and thoughts on education. The nineteenth and twentieth centuries changed the character and life-style because of the scientific innovation and technological advance. Nothing was considered to be permanent and everything seemed to be changing. This brought out a new school of thought which was known as pragmatism where a new horizon waits at the end of each vista of experience.

Summary

The philosophical basis of education thus demands the determination of certain aims and objectives. Education is a life long process, and therefore needs some frame work for its operation. It is likely that the concept of aim is associated with certain values. On an analysis of the trends in education of the east and west, it will be obvious that the basic approach to life has contributed much to the objectives set for directing Education.

Before answering the question "What are the aims of Education?" One has to come up with a definite stand on the different values and ideals concerned with education.

No doubt, ideals are connected with wishes of some people. They pick up, objectives which by definition cannot be realised in practice. Peters[1] suggests that the features of the concept of aim indicate the specific social function performed. The word "Aims" conveys first of all some suggestion of an objective that is not too near at hand or too easy to attain.

1. Peters, Rs. S., *The Philosophy of Education*, Oxford University Press, 1973, p. 13.

The main points are —

1. We tend to ask about aims in the context where we want to get people to specify more precisely what they are trying to do.
2. Aims suggest the direction of the effort towards an objective that is not too palpable or close to hand.
3. Aims also suggest the possibility of failure or of falling short.

In spite of the controversy on the desirability of aims of education one has to accept the fact that various schools of philosophy have put forward some priorities in determining the objectives. Nevertheless life and education are inseparable and, therefore, the aims of Education should have reference to the values and needs of life. In fact, the knowledge of life is essential for formulation of the aims of Education. It has been observed that human life seeks fulfilment in various ways. Its needs are different. In addition to the basic demands of life including the physical, emotional and economic needs there are cultural and spiritual necessities. Besides, man as a social being has to learn the social skills for appropriate reactions to meet the expectations of the society. Thus it is not difficult to enlist the variety of approaches to life. While determining the aims of education Dewey considers the process of development in addition to the product of education. Home says, "Education makes an individual physically, intellectually and emotionally fit to adjust in the process of life. But the question arises as to whether the aims of Education should be directed only towards adjustment or it has further aims to meet". Nunn stresses on the development of the individual self. But how would this development take place if the concept of the self remains obscure. Thus the primary objective of true education should obviously be the knowledge of the self. As emphasised by the Upanishads, every effort should be made to help an individual to know and explore the dimensions of the self. Even the importance of the development of self-concept has been acknowledged by the western psychologists like Rogers and Edwards. While the purpose of education is to discover as well as to unfold the inner self, the need for development of skills, attitudes and total personality cannot be ignored. Whitehead has attempted to strike a balance between the extreme views on the aims of Education by saying that the only object of Education is the development of a complete life. It is interesting to observe that various ideas on the aims of Education have emerged as a result of the particular emphasis laid by the individual thinker. 'Pestalozzi says "Education is the harmonious expression of physical intellectual, moral and aesthetic aspects of life". As mentioned earlier, different schools of philosophy have projected different values of life on the area of Education and brought out their significance in special contexts. While the monastic school of philosophy set priorities in the spiritual unfoldment of life, the scholastic school emphasised the role of knowledge and academic excellence. Again we find the typical approach to life and education made by the naturalistic school including Rousseau. In the opinion of Rousseau, the purpose of education is to help the individual grow in complete harmony with nature without any interference from society. This view has faced criticism from those who consider the social environment as a part of life. No matter what the priorities are, the fundamental values of life can hardly be brushed aside. Here comes the importance of the basic qualities like love, honesty, truth and goodness contributing to life itself. This view is in keeping with the idealistic approach to life. Idealism is thus not a form of realism but it makes reality more meaningful. No doubt, there still exists a confusion around the apparent conflict between realism and idealism. The purpose of Education is to synthesize both the approaches by making the best of the two. Vocational Education is considered to be the out come of this realistic approach because the socio-economic aspects of life have gained prominence at the present age.

Thus it is quite obvious that the objectives and goals of Education are determined by the needs and demands of the changing time and society. Certain perspectives and frames of reference come into picture as determinants because of their bearing on Education. Education is not a concept for picking out any specific activity. On the other hand, it is designed to lay down criteria to which a family or society must conform. There is a confusion around the differences between education and instruction. It is accepted in general that Education has a more comprehensive role and a greater responsibility. This is why its connotation is extensive and is at the same time far-reaching. Of course, the controversy exists as to whether Education as a process should be normative or otherwise. As mentioned earlier, the general criteria of education are however, laid down by the different schools of philosophy. In spite, of the angularities projected here and there certain fundamentals remain acceptable to every school. While educationists proclaim that education is of the whole man, they are no doubt, enunciating a conceptual truth. In fact, education rules out narrow specialization and a purely instrumental approach to activities. It is interesting that life and Education are almost synonymous. Living is transformed into a quality of life which constitutes the basis of Education. In this connection the approach of John Dewey deserves special mention. The analysis of both education and its aim reveals the truth that life is the core of both education and its development. The intrinsic value of Education lies in its process of unfoldment. According to the ancient wisdom, truth, beauty and goodness are interwoven in a way. The development of heart has its tremendous implication for enriching and enhancing life and education. Turning to Prof. Peters' analysis we see that he has given us three conditions as mentioned earlier. Dewey has put forward some challenging comments on the views of education and its aims. He thinks that Education cannot be related to vocation and skills. This view has been shared by many who concentrate on the fundamentals of life and mostly ignore the mundane realities.

REVIEW OF THE OBJECTIVES OF EDUCATION

It becomes obvious that the aims of education are related to the values in life. It is felt that harmony, happiness and humanity are the key-words which should offer direction in educational planning. In other words, education as a dynámic process should be oriented to all kinds of values in life. While the values differ in various contexts, life remains fundamentally progressive.

In determining the aims of education one is influenced by the different kinds of values prevalent at that time. However, the aims of education are concerned with certain fundamental concepts of life. It is not difficult to trace the history of education with reference to the specific emphasis at different times. In fact education appeared to be wedded to certain goals and remained so until the emergence of a new outlook. It was felt by a number of philosophers that education deserves autonomy and liberation from the traditional aims. New horizons flashed indicating unending and unlimited boundary for its operation. Any value may be imbibed by the young learners who should be allowed the freedom to choose their priority and standard. Nevertheless, teachers have to be careful about the evil influence of politics and its persuasion in the interest of the sanctity of education.

The changing mode of life has contributed to new modalities of perception on values. It is striking to note that the values owe their origin to the basic concepts of life and influence the system of education designed to reflect certain aims. Unfortunately, values are fluctuating today as a result of confusion about life. In order to achieve clarity and precision in the realm of values we obviously need the metaphysical approach to life. Behind matter there is, spirit behind reality and there is ultimate truth. Those in charge of planning education should have far-sightedness as well as insight to evaluate educational objectives. This is very true and is quite in keeping with the Upanishadic thoughts on education. The concept of 'paravidya' and 'aparavidya' is thus relevant to the determination of the fundamental aims of education : ''sa vidya ya vimuktaye'' is the most significant statement ever made in reference to education. Freedom from bondage of any kind is thus the ultimate goal of every human being and so of education.

The educational standard is believed to be falling at present and a few seminars have been organized and studies conducted to determine its causes. It is observed that there is no significant difference either in behaviour, attitude or in performance of the so-called educated people and uneducated. The only difference is that educated people keep more information than those who are deprived of educational opportunities. Thus education cannot guarantee any excellence today in the area of sensitivity feeling or in attitude. The reasons may, however, be attributed to confusion and conflict around aims of education. No western values could be begged or transplanted in the field of Indian education. The typical needs of India and the traits of Indian culture have to be projected on Indian education in order to make it meaningful.

FURTHER REFLECTION ON CONCEPT AND AIMS OF EDUCATION

Professor Peters defines education as initiation into a worthwhile form of life. He emphasises the evaluative aspect of the concept. It is rather difficult to come to a totally uncontroversial position regarding the formulation of aims of education. The issue is a complex one as it relates to values and their development. Education is thus a process as well as a product. Roughly speaking two types of conditions have been suggested for the use of the term education. They are desirability conditions and knowledge conditions.

Turning to Peters' analysis of aim, we see that he has emphasised three conditions, each of which has been considered as a part of the concept 'education'. Nevertheless education should have certain quality and standard in order to be meaningful. As Warnock observes, "A good education must above all things, be directed towards the strenghening of the faculty of imagination". The practical question is whether the same kind of education with the same quality can be made suitable for everyone. The answer is obviously, in the negative as the concept of quality varies to a considerable extent.

In order to attain certain roles and standard one needs a suitable curriculum for its implementation. A curriculum needs to be not only catered to the varied needs of the learners, it should also be integrated into the system with the learning process of the pupils. The teacher in the system should provide not an integration of experience, but rather those experiences which would enable the student to achieve his own integration or organisation of experience. According to Dressel,[2] the integrative process strives to organise knowledge and experience in a meaningful fashion.

---

2. Dressel, P.L., The Meaning and Significance of Integration in 57th year book of a National Society for the Study of Education, Part III.

7

ASSUMPTIONS AROUND VALUES

Assumption about values is, of all assumptions, the most important one for education, as it affects the direction of education. As in life, so in education, the question of values persists through ages. Education is believed to be a purposive activity towards ends which are deemed to be good. While some aims of education are universally agreed upon, others are controversial. There is a wide divergence between aims and it is a challenging task to reconcile them with confidence.

Philosophy of education should, show the implications for education with reference to beliefs in values. The beliefs vary but they are not mutually exclusive.

Beliefs about Values

There are some educational values which we take for granted at first sight as desirable, depending upon our beliefs. The effect of such values on education is obvious enough. The practice and thought of education are affected by assumptions of many kinds. Practice is illuminated by thinking. Assumptions about values affect the direction of the moral guidance we give, they also affect the direction of the curriculum, attitudes and personality as well.

It is, however, worthwhile to compare values for the sake of a critical analysis. Perhaps we cannot finally settle the progress towards the truth which can be evaluated by judgement of values.

Our main concern here is with the values in education. Education is a part of life. Therefore, our questions about values in education are inseparable from larger questions of values in life. In short, values are embodied in education and educational practice. Value is a term applied to an actual complex factual state of affairs to which we attach the adjective 'valuable'. The normal use of the term is positive rather than negative. But this is too narrow a concept.

Three Ways of Comparing Values

The word 'value' may mean in the broadest sense any object or state of affairs which satisfies desire, gives pleasure or satisfaction of any kind. This is rather a descriptive sense of 'value'. It is a face value and in this sense there is no distinction between lower and higher values.

We may compare values in a normative way in which things, morally good, are opposed to things which are morally bad. Here we believe that we ought to cultivate one set of values and ought to avoid the others. Comparison is also possible between pairs of values in which they are not opposed as good versus bad. In the third place, we may compare values with one another without judging the relative merits on a relative scale. One value may be put side by side in a particular perspective. Thus the values of possessing and exercising skills may be put side by side with the value of health.

Types of Values Analysed

If we return to the first basis of comparison, viz., the morally normative comparison in which 'ought' is opposed to 'ought not', it would be desirable though formidable, to determine the priority of each value. In the widest sense, values are objects of satisfaction. But desires and satisfactions which are not morally supported cannot serve as a sound criterion. We do believe that there is an invariable connection between 'truly good' and what is most deeply satisfying to human beings. They are seen to be two faces of the same thing, a pattern and quality of total human living. It should, however, be noted that this accounts for a thorough search for a wider ground of human good. The particular idea or concept of ideas of what is good to do and seek must change along with other changes within the social structure.

Thus there are other sets of values besides moral, which cannot be lost sight of. Let us consider a few things which cannot be brushed aside in the contemporary world as unimportant in life and education. Some of the values are more immediate ones, relative to immediate individual and social needs. Others are less immediate and more general. Some of them are moral while some are religious. Some are both means and ends, and a few claim to be ends only.

For the sake of convenience they may be classified as follows:

(a) Values agreed as basis of individual and social living:

(b) Values broadly agreed to by educationists in western democracy;

(c) Values which are under dispute; and

(d) Values held to be important by special schools of thought.

Under the first heading, some of the basic skills are considered to be necessary for obvious social reasons. Then there is a need for development of personality in a democracy which may come under category (b) Besides, there are those which are almost projections of personal or group temperament. There are other value beliefs which are not so obviously connected with temperament and which yet seem to be influenced by it. One example is the emphasis in education upon intellectual development as distinct from concern with feelings and attitude. One can often sense in a modern school the emphasis on personality development and social awareness.

Justification of Judgements of Values

These are some of the many value beliefs involved in education. The question arises how we justify judgements of value and how we reason and argue about them. The conflict is not between values higher or lower. In fact, we are concerned with its multiplicity of values, making various claims upon us. Every now and then, we are called upon to make choices. On what principles do we choose when there is a conflict? Can we decide about values in a rational and objective manner? Can any one come up with single key to find a solution or is there a hierarchy of values ruled by some supreme ordering principle?

In short, "Is there any final truth about values based on our judgements"? The attack on the objectivity of ethical knowledge arose out of logical positivism. In fact ethical statements are neither analytic nor empirical and are thus unverifiable. An ethical judgement is not based on pure fact as it involves a certain kind of emotion. The various forms of subjectivism have made it clear how closely ethical judgements are related to feeling. There is a need for effective involvement as well as objectivity, but it is extremely difficult to achieve it. But this objectivity is not detached from the self and our progress from within. It is a sincere attempt to get beyond our own private limitations in one way. Yet, I am thinking more objectively. Secondly. it is the conception of what ought to be, which is subject to change.

The Problem of the Hierarchy of Values

With these preliminary questions it is worthwhile to consider some substance or content of competing claims between different values in life and education. The question arises as to whether there is any key principle which can give overruling guidance in moral and educational judgement and decisions.

Concluding Observations

The following theme may be followed for studying values and value-oriented education:

(1) Concept of Value and Value Orientation Form — (a) Philosophical, (b) Psychological and (c) Sociological perspectives;

(2) Science, Technology and Values;

(3) Value Education: Inculcation of Values; and

(4) Teacher Education for Value-inculcation.

VALUES AND VALUE-ORIENTATION

In the determination of human behaviour the most important factor is people's specific value awareness. One's choice of the course of action is dependent on the value alternatives. We prefer one course of action to another on our assumption that our choice will help to realize our values to a higher degree.

Changes occur in a person's value perception. For human quality improvement we are required to modify some of our values and identify the ways in which such modification can be developed. It is also required to have the ideal of soundness of the values to which we subscribe and build our value systems. This can be achieved through value orientation. Education is not merely a systematic process of transferring skill, it also imparts the rationale for value orientation and provides strategies for value clarification towards human development. Thus people's ability to respond to varying and demanding situations would develop adequately. We may however, follow a three-fold method to judge the soundness of our values: (a) by identifying the developments which constitute the realization of the currently dominating values we subscribe to, (b) by isolating factors which tend to preserve or determine such values, and (c) thirdly, by providing strategies and techniques for retaining the degree of such values.

In this context what is most important is to identify the values of a person or a society. The knowledge of the value structure, and the dynamics of value orientation is imperative.

Before proceeding further with the subject it is necessary to make an attempt to place some general definition of 'value' The simplest way to understand 'value' is the economic value theory that is exchange or market value of a commodity. It is not also difficult to understand that we value an object or a job that fulfils our 'needs' and 'wants'. Social value reflects an empirical content that some social groups may achieve to motivate social action. A value also denotes some idealism like patriotism, Leelfless service, environmental conservation, non-violence and so on.

Values mean the cherished end-states and the awareness of actions that directs human endeavour. Values also help to decide legitimate goals, which set in social actions. Values also indicate truth, good beauty and freedom and the inherent human drive for realizing these values. These are accepted as spiritual values.

'Value' indicates a persisting code or standard. It determines how people can order the thrust of their desire for various jobs, actions, ways of life, etc. It is a continuum of prescriptive and proscriptive forces having a sense of reliability, depending on culturally acquired or transmitted attitudes.

MAN IN EDUCATION

Human Nature

Man is endowed with a number of faculties. He has a soul, body and a mind. He possesses a number of faculties. He functions in a number of ways by exercising his cognitive, affective and conative domains. Besides, reasoning, thinking and judgement are his main assets. He is also guided by his feelings and emotions.

Man has his social and spiritual selves as well. He has his intelligence and power of adoptation. He explores, experiment, and manipulates the environment. Besides, he has the creative abilities as well. As a creative being man functions and shapes his environment. He has various roles and responsibilities.

MAN AND HIS PURPOSE OF LIFE

It is a controversial issue as the purpose is different in different contexts. Very often we hear about the spiritual aim of life. Man has come to this world mainly to fulfil his ambitions of self-realisation. It is also felt that this cannot be the only objective for a man in the society. He has got his social roles and responsibilities. So it is wrong for him to ignore this important part of life. Of course, there is a question of priority and he has to choose between various aims according to the situation and context.

Throughout the ages, man's quest for truth has been marked by the various events in the socio-religious history of mankind. Right from the Upanishadic age, we find different modalities of expression in the spiritual life and socio-political spheres. One wonders as to the preference of one to another.

Man has been described by Sir Alexis Carrel as the 'unknown'. According to him, he is the most mysterious creature on earth. Regarding the concept of manhood it may be said that it is a stage to the reached through persistent effort. It is not the physical appearance which is important in a man. It is his mind and spirit which are the main sources of his identity. The scientific basis of evolution does not explain the entire process of self promotion. Yet, the theory of evolution as propounded by Darwin at least shows the possibility of man's immense potential to develop and grow in all directions. In the *Life Divine* written by Sri Aurobindo, it has been pointed out that man may reach the supramental stage or enter into a divine life by means of meditation and yogic process. Similarly, mind and life cannot grow into their fullness except by the opening of the large and greater consciousness to which mind only approaches.

Humanity and manhood are related no doubt, but they are not the same. The finer sentiments and qualities of heart and head are considered to be very important factors contributing to humanity. One the other hand, manhood is a term which is more operational. It includes the idea of development and growth, which can be cultivated with deliberation. Man becomes more mature and determined to reach perfection by dint of his own effort. Thus the concept of man is multi-dimensional.

The cognitive growth of man is no less important than his emotional development. Both interact is a mysterious way to make the functioning more effective.

In order to explain the concept of man it will be better to cite certain examples. In the history of mankind we find all types of people. Some are bold, heroic, while some are timid and weak. In the same way we can classify people in different groups, according to their appearance, strength, quality, interest and attitude. We have found Buddha, Chaitanya and Gandhi. At the same time, we find Hitler and Mussoline. Thus, the man manifests himself in various ways and lifestyles. It is interesting that the characteristics of man may be fundamentally similar in all lands at all ages. Yet, the variation we notice among them reminds us of the diversity in creation.

Man is also known by his performance, as a tree is known by its fruits. Man is known by his character personality and a distinctive flavour. With all this he faces this life and places himself in a particular position for further development. No one rests at the same point as life is a continuous development. Therefore, we find different correlates of manhood, like environment, society, community and education.

According to the clinical psychology, man has a lot of imperfections within him. Yet he is the best in the creation. He is rational. The rational part of the man elevates his human existence and shows him the way to divinity. Nevertheless, his frailties and irrational self create a lot of conflicts within him. The Freudian concept of man is, of course, not very optimistic about human perfection. To him the primitive self cannot be denied and there is constant struggle going on in every human heart. The ego or the social self has been emphasized by a lot of psychologists for practical purpose. It is perhaps realistic to believe in the dynamic nature of man and the angularities of each human being. Thus it is extremely difficult to come up with a single notion of man because of the multiplicity of characteristics within him. It is unfortunate that man in spite of his continuous struggle has been at the same point for ages. No matter how much advancement he has made in the field of technology and science, his basic nature has not changed much. He remains a mystery forever.

Man stands as incomplete being in the life-long process of education. It is the task of education to build up the concept of man and develop in him the values for transfer from generation to generation. It is quite obvious that culture is like a flowing river which changes its course from time to time. Yet, it contributed substantially to human civilisation. Man as a unique part of the creation has a peculiar position. On the one hand he has his role as an architect of his future. On the other hand, he is subservient to the needs of the society, and thus, his responsibility is unending. His complex mode of behaviour suggests the scope for modification of his knowledge and skill as well as the attitude for better adjustment to community life. It is quite usual to think that there is a need for attention and recognition in human life. This is the basic requirement.Modes of behaviour which serve to satisfy his needs are very varied. They are built up in course of life.

As mentioned earlier the importance of manhood has been acknowledged at various ages by different cross-sections of people. The observations of a number of intellectuals have clarified the concept of man in terms of operational variable. It is not very uncommon to admit the narrowness of the logical frame of reference with its limits. Man's behaviour is developed through reinforcement. More frequently the reinforcement takes place, the better the pattern of behaviour. In education today we find that some desirable behaviour patterns also develop along with undesirable behaviour traits. The reduction of undesirable behaviour patterns can only be achieved through reinforcements of his good behaviour. It is quite usual to instil in the children the ideas of love and humanity from the very beginning in order to make a child a worthy citizen of the world. It goes without saying that the need for education is now imperative and the term education is used in a very popular sense.

If we sum up, we can observe the following:

1. Man should be at the centre of any educational programme.
2. The concept of man should be well formulated with reference to his roles and responsibilities.
3. The changing perspectives and the modern lifestyle should be considered at the time of educational planning for the development of humanity.
4. The methods of humanising education and socializing man should be innovated.
5. As man should be the prime concern in any educational programme, so our life should be the source of stimulation and education.

8

CURRENT TRENDS IN EDUCATION

Education has emerged as a separate discipline in recent times. It draws materials from a number of subject areas and is considered as an interdisciplinary approach.

It has developed in various perspectives with new dimensions. It has shifted its emphasis on child and its needs to start with. The process of teaching and learning has been analysed for evolving a scientific basis of education. The interaction model has gained its prominence among all and group dynamics have been introduced in classroom teaching. Teachers' role has been widened and the function of a teacher is not limited to classroom teaching. The emerging concept of child development has influenced education and child rearing practices. Teaching no longer means imparting instruction. It involves 'give and take' action and interaction. Exploration and experimentation have been considered as the main techniques of education.

Micro-teaching and macro-teaching have been introduced for diagnostic purpose to improve teaching. The various traits and characteristics of good teaching have been kept as criteria for comparing the qualities of teaching. Beside the concept of curriculum has recently changed. Providing knowledge and experience in different subject-areas has become the goal of framing a comprehensive curriculum. It is flexible and not rigid, total and not isolated.

Interdisciplinary approach has been introduced to integrate the areas of knowledge and experience. School has been regarded as a miniature society — a community centre.

Lastly, evaluation has replaced examination. It involves evaluation of personality, knowledge and performances by means of observation and testing. While education is a means of socialization it enriches the social and cultural life of an individual and society In fine, education has currently been more experimental than before. It is engaged in exploration of new dimensions and dynamics for the improvement of standard in general.

DEMOCRACY AS A CURRENT TREND IN EDUCATION

Education is a social process and this concept of education has been evolved gradually. The criterion for educational criticism and construction implies a particular social ideal. A society, which makes provision for participation in the good of all its members on equal terms and which secures flexible readjustment of its institution through interaction of the different forms of associated life, is democratic. Such a society must have a type of education which offers interest in social relationship and control.

Education has been considered as a means for complete and harmonious development of all powers with reference to the needs of a humanitarian goal. The national as well as social background has influenced the development of democratic concept of education to a great extent. On the one hand, the individual freedom has been granted for a fuller, freer and more fruitful association and intercourse of all human beings while on the other, a wider social aim for a democratic society has been kept in view. This appears to create some conflicts so far as the interfusion of these two goals is concerned. The conclusion is, however, bound up with the very idea of education as an unfoldment of individual capacity in progressive growth directed to social aims. According to Dewey, education as such has no aims. An educational aim must be founded upon the instrinsic activities and needs in a changing society. As a preparation of life, education has got to suggest the kind of environment needed to liberate and organise individual capacities.

Pragmatism and Democracy

To Dewey, there can be no ultimate aims of education as the imposition of certain aims on education might render the work of both teacher and pupil mechanical and slavish. So far as the sources of education are concerned, Dewey differs to some extent from his predecessors like Rousseau who says, "We receive from three sources — nature, men and thing". Dewey emphasised experience as a positive source. These experiences when brought together constitute education and stimulate living. Education has its function to create learning situation for generating and enriching experiences. To Dewey, "experience shared is experience enriched". He has also suggested method of sharing experiences. To Dewey, school is neither a family nor a state, it is a miniature society where the pupils learn together by common participation in a variety of learning situations. The philosophy behind the democracy is mainly humanitarian. It ensures equality of opportunity and freedom for the development of the whole man through happiness. It is, however, criticised that under the democratic ideals brighter pupils are sacrificed and opportunity is provided more for the less bright pupils in relation to their capacities.

On a critical review it will be observed that Dewey's concept of democracy in education has its limitations as well. Experience in education is the key word in Dewey's concept and it consists of the active relations existing between human beings and his natural and social surroundings. But this experience is hardly crystallised in a set up which does not demand any thing more towards the goal. Thus teacher, in Dewey's democratic concept, is nothing more than a part of the environment. His function is only to stimulate the group relationship for distribution of experiences. He has not a very distinct role so as to direct the activities of the pupils for gathering experiences and this leads to wastage in education. Efficiency has been presupposed in Dewey's democratic set up and rich human materials expected. In actual practice things are far from what were conceived by Dewey. So far as curriculum is concerned nothing fixed has been set except some broad categories for generating experiences which are the raw materials of education. This again demands high efficiency both amongst individual pupils as well as teachers. Thus school as a miniature society very often fails to provide those experiences as envisaged by Dewey. Nevertheless Dewey's concept of democracy in education has its outstanding merits. It has at least revitalised the stale and stagnant, rather the static concept of education as a mechanical process. No wonder that Dewey with certain amount of optimism has faced a challenging situation pregnant with all possibilities.

Democracy in Education

Democracy has become the slogan of the day in the field of education. It opens up a new road to the question of social organisation, to the question of freedom in school. It has emphasised the need for examining our cultural heritage and human values. Thus democracy besides, being a method is also a faith or a theory of value or social philosophy. Dewey puts forward his concept of democracy in education as a challenge to the rigid and conservative outlook. His democracy means a free healthy climate where full sharing of interest within a group becomes possible. It is thus a grand ideal, a way of life, a philosophical point of view hardly to be dispensed with.

Democracy is essentially a process of determining the values governing individual and social choices. It is a theory in operation and when operating, it becomes a norm of action. It is made of conjoint associated living where science, education and the democratic cause meet as one. It is obvious that the relation between democracy and pragmatism is a reciprocal one. Democracy is itself an educational principle or policy. It is a comprehensive plan for the organisation for individual and collective conduct. Thus democracy values experience and experimentation. Both democracy and experimentation are similar in many ways. One demands unending research and the other a continuous catering of interest.

The modern movement in education known as the new education rests upon the basic principles of democracy which accepts everyone as being one of the people. In other words, democracy as a principle believes in equality and freedom. It is a fact that there are certain imperfections of democracy. Still it contains within itself the possibility of progress. Living and learning go-together where democracy prevails. It is not enough that young people should have passively absorb the accepted values of life. They should also have direct experience through education. The variety of life situations should foster a spirit of democracy which evolves itself under congenial atmosphere. There are various facts of democracy, viz., political, economic, personal and spiritual. The larger the need for living together in peace, the greater would be the scope for democracy. The function of an educationist is to foster the growth of world democracy. If a school is to grow into a community, the first essential condition is the happy relation between the members of the school. Education is a process of nurturing this democratic ideal by promoting friendship and community spirit. It makes possible the emergence of truth, beauty and goodness, if there is no external pressure. Authoritarian outlook has every chance to hinder the progress of democracy, and as such the authoritarians are the worst enemies of the democratic way of life.

If one believes in democracy, he shall seek to promote freedom in and through the family and to help parents build personalities.

Thus education has a responsibility towards building up a system whereby the members of a community live together and can give the maximum service to the community. It is possible that democracy is not something that can be bestowed or given. It is essentially to be earned through knowledge and consideration, liberty and dignity of the individual man. Democracy does not, therefore, know where it is going but only feels its way.

Education is a means to the fulfilment of this dream, yet to be realised. Where democracy is an adventure education is the resource. According to Whitehead, "The primary objective must be to get pupils to acquire the values which underlie the democratic system. There is a great deal of philosophical and other work to be done here on what the precise content of teaching should be".

Whitehead says that there can be no successful democratic society till general education conveys a philosophic outlook. Democracy presupposes non-interference and rests upon the varying and changing values of life. It is related to pragmation and thrives on diversity. Education today is, therefore, more interested in dispensing with the rigid notion and authoritarian outlook. Full freedom should be ensured with a view to attaining the goal. This has influenced the various factors of education. The methodology and classroom situation have been reviewed in the light of the democratic goals and in short, the human factors in education have been correlated through democracy.

Where culture is the flower of civilisation, democracy is its fruition. As a principle, it has its appeal though as a practice it is not free from limitations. Nevertheless democracy finds itself reflected in various spheres of education. Teacher's function has been formulated keeping in view the ideals of democracy. He is regarded as a friend, philosopher and guide and he has the responsibility to act as a link between school and society. The curriculum has been so framed as to contain the elements of humanity and universal brotherhood. The role of community life in education has also been increased in the present programme. So far as the method of teaching is concerned, it is almost certain that pupils' experience has been taken into full account in classroom activities. It has been accepted that pupils can learn and profit more by sharing their experiences by way of discussions, than by any other means. This approach, no doubt, shows a respect for the individuality of each pupil expressed through modification of methodology on democratic principles. As regards, the last but not the least important factor, i.e., examination, it must be admitted that evaluation of the total personality of a child is the prime concern of modern education. It is the totality of a man which counts and in the present crisis one cannot think of education without any reference to world citizenship. Thus democracy as a philosophy has been accepted without much hesitation in the educational systems of the day.

Overview

Democracy, is thus a dynamic concept. It is very difficult to explain the term and clarify the modern concepts without its systematic analysis. The concept of democracy, has been changing from age to age or from place to place. In spite of the fact, it has brought about new modes of living. It has acquired vast popularity all over the world on the ground that it manifests equity, and social justice for peaceful co-existence in the fast-changing world of our time.

According to a number of writers, democratic ways of life can be traced back on the primitive age; it had its origin in the 'State of Nature'. There had been equality in the true sense only in those days and fraternal bond within the same tribe was quite natural. There are indications of peaceful co-existence and harmony with nature.

Even in ancient Greece, democracy was a form of government in which every citizen, had a direct share and positive role in deliberation and legislative processes.

With the passage of time, the medieval history stepped into Renaissance with the dawn of modern times. The products of Renaissance culture are obviously secularism, liberalism and individualism. All these forces naturally found expression in humanism, and this tended to bring about harmony and democratic ideals in social life and also in education.

"Humanism," according to Hans, implies "both a human and a humane" approach to educational problems. "It is human in the sense that human nature and human interests should not be suppressed; it is humane in the sense that the nature of the child and its growing mind should not be suppressed. This concept fertilised the soil for sowing the seeds of democracy. This indicates that social harmony and peace can be arrived through freedom.

Contradictions

In the words of Lowell, 'Democracy is an experiment in government; further, it may be a type of state and an order of society'. Maxey opines that democracy is not merely a political formula. It is a search for a way of life. It is the belief that such a way of life is the best way for all mankind. Democracy does not necessarily mean that all individuals are alike or equal. It tends to eliminate the apparent contradictory principles. Every member in the community may be entitled to attain the highest goal possible for him, through democracy.

Role of Education in Democracy

The success of democracy, depends upon the rational attitude of the group members or the common people which, in turn, depends upon the development of personal qualities of individuals. Education has, therefore, a definite role to play in this sphere. It tends to imbibe the art of good life through manifestation of peace and harmony. Democracy represents a philosophy of life or a way of ideal living in any social group. It stands for certain claims and opportunities that direct toward the way of a 'good life'. It is natural, therefore, that education must have some broad objectives and aspirations for the attainment of such a good life. The major dimensions of these democratic objectives are stated below:

(a) Liberty and Freedom;

(b) Equality of Opportunity;

(c) Protection of Human Rights;

(d) Decentralisation;

(e) Fraternity in Human Relationship and Peaceful Co-existence; and

(f) Unity and Social Harmony.

Analysis of Objectives in the Context of Educational Principles

(a) Democracy is to safeguard liberty and freedom of expression. It becomes baseless in the absence of this freedom. It helps to manifest the perfections in man. It further promotes liberty in the choice of one's vocation or courses of studies according to interest and ability.

(b) In the second place, democracy must ensure equality of opportunity for every individual. This may be achieved through abolition of class distinctions or social disparity and injustice. In any case, the fundamental goal of democracy is attainment of equality, and harmony at all levels. This objective asserts that education should be the birth right of all, irrespective of caste, colour, sex, rank or economic status. It further asserts that there should be free and compulsory elementary education up to a certain age, and free social education for non-literate adult and deprived population. Obviously, there should exist common schooling as against class-education.

(c) Besides, in democracy human rights are protected for growth and development. These rights are protected not only for fostering individual qualities but also for enriching social development. For this reason, importance of recognition of individual worth by fostering proper means of stimulation becomes so indispensable.

It is our common experience that any form of democratic organisation consists of heterogeneous social groups. So, diversities and disintegrative forces must be there. Each of these divergent groups has a unique social contributive property of its own. Some are intellectually advanced, some are physically strong, some are promising and prone to any type of adventurous activities while others are adaptive to various socio-political or cultural situations. Democracy nourishes the best qualities of all the divergent groups — big or small, advanced or backward. The main object of democracy is to establish a harmonious relationship amongst these various social groups and active unity in the midst of these diversities. An educational institution is also a democratic organisation in democratic countries. It consists of innumerable social groups of varing characteristics. However, the educational institution creates conditions leading to self development and self-realisation of its group members and unfolds the hidden genius kept dormant within these social groups. All these qualities, taken as a whole, constitute a unique corporate life, they develop a sort of concert or harmony and augment the qualities of the institution and of the society. So, diversities are the ingredients of social harmony and greater unity. This harmony and unity are achieved through democratic ideals of education. It is for this reason, great thinkers like Rabindranath Tagore, M.K. Gandhiji and Vivekananda assigned much importance on unity of mankind.

9

FREEDOM AND DISCIPLINE

Freedom is a word used in various contexts. It has different connotations. It is a condition of human living, a particular state of mind but it is not licence. It is a concept which is opposite to the concept of bondage.

It is sometimes used in a negative sense. Yet it may be positive. However controversial the term may be, it refers to certain values. Freedom in the first and the basic sense means freedom from restrictions, and all kinds of constraints. It also implies salvation which demies laws and conventions, fears and restraints. Even freedom ignores impulse inhibition. It is wonderful to have freedom which is, no doubt, enhanced by values. If life is a prison we are all prisoners. Is it then possible to have freedom? This is an intriguing question. Obviously freedom leads to happiness which comes from within. It is believed that complete detachment is the condition for freedom. In 'Geeta' it has been stated that the person who has the capacity to control his impulses has the potential to enjoy freedom. In other words, without freedom happiness cannot be won. This particular issue of freedom is rather complex. The questions of fact are mainly two — What are we free from? and What are we limited by? The more interesting question of value is what do we want to be free from, and why? In short, the question of freedom revolves round the concept of values. It is assumed that freedom is good itself. It is also true that freedom in its prime sense is neither good nor bad. It is a neutral fact. Thus freedom is a compound idea which stands for a number of conditions and states of mind. It is neither good nor bad but factual. The significance of freedom lies in its use. It can be internal or external. The primary notion of freedom from restraint has a reference to the ethics. The traditional concepts of freedom of will and the freedom of choice are somewhat interrelated.

The ideas of freedom and determination may be examined by the two questions as follows: (1) Are we free to choose? and (2) To what extent are we free to do so? Freedom to do this or that, to do or not to do is of great moral importance. If we are not free, the question of morality does not arise. Can this freedom be philosophically justified? Whatever may be the answer it is true that the freedom is a condition for discipline. We are, of course, influenced to a great extent, by heredity and environment, by temperament and character. If this is so then how could we be completely free? Does this mean that our freedom is limited? In fact, we are free to choose or not to choose within certain limits. We blame mankind for its inconsistency but we are to remember that there is a destiny or fate which play vital roles in our life. It is, however, too difficult to deny destiny but it is not impossible to create our own fate.

The question of freedom is thus related to other issues. Human beings have been endowed with reasoning which helps him to distinguish the right from the wrong, the good from the bad. It is a power, a capacity to judge the values for the right choice. A freedom is, however, not the same as liberty. We have our own limits and limitations, as discussed. Freedom from external and internal restraints and freedom of the will are not the same as liberty. Another dimension of freedom emerges as a result of the exercise of the freedom when in conflict. This can be discovered not only in moral living but through the acceptance of the discipline of learning.

To attain freedom is a supreme end of education. Freedom of a child is the first word of child-centered education. Without freedom personality cannot grow spontaneously, Kart held that all moral acts are not free acts. "Freedom is the truth of necessity," says Hegel. It is a compliance with a law, which is in conformity with our highest nature. According to Kant, in moral action the individual is obeying a law coming from the self. Within there is a categorical imperative. The transcendental freedom of Kant is not accepted by Harbert. Education would be tyranny if it did not lead to freedom. Freedom may be used as freedom from external strain or freedom of will or choosing freedom from conformity to order. According to professor Reid, freedom is mental detachment. Dewey mentions positive freedom which involves social guidance. Discipline on the other hand is related to freedom. It consists in the submission of one's impulses and power to a regulation. It is something some control applied upon the people for getting obedience. There is a misconception that freedom is opposed to discipline. As mentioned earlier, freedom and discipline are interdependent. Nunn says that discipline is not external, it touches the inmost springs of conduct. It controls and vibrates all our emotions and thoughts and gives perfect shape to all our activities. Freedom and discipline are not opposed to each other. Bertrand Russell says, "True discipline is not externally controlled but it is spontaneous and it leads to perfect development". John Dewey is also of the opinion that discipline brings social control. In short, freedom and discipline are two sides of the same coin. Freedom could not be used properly without discipline and discipline cannot be enforced without certain degree of freedom. Discipline, according to Herbert, is a continuous process which resorts to punishment. Freedom in a condition for effective discipline and discipline is the product of freedom. On a critical analysis we find that discipline can be considered as a concept in the sense of control. It may mean self discipline which is involved in exercising one's freedom and joy. One must be reasonably free from external restraint for maintaining the discipline without any imposition. There is also a literal sense of discipline, which comes from the word disciple. It naturally means submission, service and acceptance.

Discipline is connected with disciples, with pupils, with learning.

The art of discipline is the art of making disciples. The word 'discipline' acquires two meanings: (a) Restrictive treatment by teachers and (b) order among pupils achieved by this kind of treatment.

Thus the word has been changing its connotation from time to time.

Sometimes it means orderly conduct which is a social matter while in another context it implies moral values and correction. According to comprehensive dictionary meaning, discipline is an orderly action by instructing, them in the same way.

Another meaning of the word is the orderly conduct and action which result from training.

It is apparent that the word 'discipline' has become almost depersonalized. Discipline begins with a natural desire to achieve some goal in the realms of truth, beauty or goodness in personal or community life. The essence of real discipline is thus, not forced submission.

Discipline and freedom grow together. They are mutually interdependent. There are two kinds of discipline — One is positive while the other is negative. One refers to generation of best human impulses and their application. The use of the word discipline is, however, different from popular usage in which the word may mean either stern treatment or orderly behaviour. Discipline is thus a state of mind but order is a state of affairs.

Summary

The word 'freedom' is used in different contexts. Originally it comes from the word free and is a condition for living. Freedom is also the birth-right of every human being. Man is born free. Nobody likes interference. Thus it is a basic condition for effective functioning. "Freedom is a basic need," Kant says that all moral acts may not be free acts. There are limits to freedom. In short, freedom may imply both positive and negative concepts. For example, freedom from want and fear is more positive as a concept. Similarly freedom for self-expression has also a positive implication. Freedom in education has a wide connotation. This implies freedom of action on the part of teachers and parents, in school and classroom, at home and in the community. Thus freedom is a relative term. It goes without saying that freedom and self-control are not contradictory. Control of self is imperative for getting the full benefit of freedom. In other words, discipline enhances the scope of freedom. Discipline implies self-restraint.

10

CREATIVITY AND THE ROLE OF EDUCATION

The concept of creativity emerged in Europe during the period of renaissance and it was first formally used by the philosophers. The term was originally used to indicate the "great analogy" between the divine creator of the natural world and the artist with his power to create "forms which were never in Nature".

Today creativity is generally considered as the ability to make or bring into existence something new. It may be a new solution to a problem, a new method or device or a new artistic object or form. Sometimes it is also understood as a particular ability in action. Thus creativity is a specific ability. It has both a potential and functional side.

An enormous amount of research is being conducted on creativity in the West, particularly in U.S.A., but little conceptual agreement has been reached on what creativity is. When it is conceived by one group as a specific ability to create something new, others think of it not as an ability but rather as a psychological process by which noble and valuable products are created.

The third group considers creativity not as a process but as the product. Actually the definitions that are put forward to explain creativity ranges from simple problem solving to actualisation of self. In spite of all the differences of opinions about the nature of creativity, agreement is reached at least on one point that creativity is not a theoretical construct. It is a general traint which can be subjected to a variety of evaluative criteria.

To do justice to all the ideas and concepts associated with creativity there is a need to analyse and evaluate the perspectives such as (i) creativity as an ability or (ii) creative situation, (iii) the creative process, and (iv) the creative product. All these complete the facets of creativity as conceived today.

1. Creative Ability

A large number of research studies was conducted in U.S.A. and many other countries to identify the nature and characteristics of creative ability through inquiries into the activities of the creative people of distinction. The researches reveal that creative persons are people of high intelligence.

It was noticed that there is high correlation between intelligence and creativity up to certain level (e.g., I.Q. of 120-130) but beyond that, the correlation is not so high. That is, people of high I.Q. (above 150) are not found to be highly creative and highly creative persons generally do not possess very high I.Q. as the term implies. Eminent psychologist like Guilford conducted researches on creative ability and found that the intelligence tests constructed prior to 1950 do not consider all the components of creative ability. It was found that high creative ability does not always bear high positive correlation with superior intelligence.

A great deal of research has been carried out on the nature, incidence and cultivation of creativity, particularly, by U.S. psychologists (and later by Russian psychologists) since the World War II. It was believed that creative ability is normally distributed like intelligence and attempts were made by psychometricians to develop tests that measure creative abilities. Those involve test items such as multiple word associations, composition of fable endings, description of unusual uses or improvements for ordinary objects or implements. Power of novelty, is considered as an essential component of creative ability and is an inducement to action as established by psychological experiments.

Creative ability has the following characteristics:

(i) Creative ability involves production of new and original ideas.

(ii) It comes as a sudden flash.

(iii) Creative ability leads to perception of new relationship in a unique way.

(iv) It involves production of unique and useful things.

(v) It is often associated with tension in terms of such dualities as intellect and intuition, the conscious and unconscious, mental health and mental disorder, the conventional and unconventional, complexity and simplicity, symmetry and asymmetry, and psychological balance and imbalance.

(vi) Creative ability sometimes involves immature personality traits which may be an extension of a generalised receptivity to a wider than normal range of experience and behaviour patterns.

(vii) It leads to exceptionally deep, awareness of the self.

(viii) Creative ability turns those who have it to be more primitive and more cultured, more destructive and more constructive, madder and saner than average persons.

A research study into the nature and activities of a large number of creative persons of distinction reveal that a productively creative person is dominant, possessed of those qualities and attributes that underlie and lead to achievement of personal status, although not of a specially sociable or participative temperament, but demanding, aggressive and self-centred outlook. He is, permissive and verbally fluent, self confident and self assured and relativity uninhibited in expressing his worries and complaints.

Creative persons are comparatively free from conventional restraints and inhibitions and not preoccupied with the impression they make on others. Thus they are capable of great independence and autonomy and are relatively ready to recognise and admit self views that are unusual and unconventional. They are strongly motivated to achieve in situations in which independence in thought and action is called for. A creative person is not inclined to strive for achievement in settings where conforming behaviour is expected or required. He is efficient and steady in intellectual efforts.

2. Creative Situation

Creativity is not a fixed trait of personality. It is something that changes overtime. But there can hardly be any agreement in respect of specifying types of situation or life circumstances that facilitate or inhibit creativity. The reason is that it is unlikely that all persons will find the same situation equally conducive to creative effort. Falling of an apple from the tree on the ground could only move Isaac Newton's creativity to discover the law of gravitation. So many people jump into the full-to-the brim bathtub or cistern but it is only Archimedes who is creatively motivated to discover the laws of floatation. An inquiry into the life history of greatly creative persons reveal the widest variety of early circumstances and family situations which in different ways contributed to their growth as a creative individual. A nation-wide research study in U.S.A. on creativity inquired into the life history and important episodes of a large number of highly creative architects to identify the specific circumstances and situations which facilitate creativity and which retard it. The findings of that research study disclosed that the following situations and conditions fostered creativity in those architects:

1. An extraordinary respect by the parent for the child and an early granting to him usual freedom in exploring his universe and in making his own decisions.
2. An expectation that the child would not act independently but reasonably and responsibly.
3. A lack of intense closeness between the parent and the child so that neither own dependence is encouraged nor a feeling of rejection is experienced. In other words, the sort of interpersonal relationship between the parent and the child has a liberating effect upon the child.
4. A plentiful supply of models in the extended social environment of the child for identification and promotion of his ego ideals.
5. The presence of clear standard of conduct and ideas as to what is right and what is wrong, in the family and at the same time an expectation, if not requirement, of active exploration and internalisation of a framework of personal conduct.
6. An emphasis upon the development of an individual ethical code: the experience of frequent moving within the community as well as from community to community, country to country which provides richness of experience both personal and cultural and adds at the same time a feeling of loneliness, shyness, isolation and solitariness in childhood and adolescence.
7. Freedom to achieve skill and abilities at their own pace and encouragement and reward for the same by the parents and relatives in the society, and
8. Absence of pressure on the child to establish prematurely his professional identity.

It cannot be guaranteed that all these factors will be equally helpful to the development of creativity in persons, engaged in other occupations and in countries other than U.S.A. But it is undeniable that many of these are conducive to the growth of creativity in persons engaged in different occupations in all countries including India. A look into the boyhood experiences of Rabindranath Tagore reveals that most of these situations and conditions were prevalent in his early life and it might be that these helped his growth as a great creator.

3. The Creative Process

The creative process is the set of activities both mental and physical, involving our individual and social senses and leading to innovations, discoveries, inventions and creation in fields of human knowledge. It starts from sensing of a need or experiencing a deficiency and passes through the stages of exploration, clarification, preparation, formulation, experimentation and evaluation of what has been achieved through experiment. The creative process has the following distinct phases:

(a) *Preparatory Phase* : This phase of the creative process begins when a person after experiencing a need or deficiency is motivated to reach a solution. During this phase one acquires the knowledge, skill and technique associated with the need or problem through which he visualises the pros and cons of the problem or need.

(b) The second phase is a phase of concentrated attention in any attempt to solve the problem. During this phase attention is focussed solely upon the problem until it is solved. Some time at this stage there may be blocking of one's efforts to solve the problem and experiencing of frustration, tension and discomfort. One is led to such discomfort, tension and frustration for sheer self protection, i.e., protection of his service or occupation, prestige or dignity, etc.

(c) The third phase is a period of withdrawal from the problem. It is a kind of psychological going out of the field, a period of renunciation of the problem or recession from it. It is actually the inculcation period which often leads to insight for success or solution of the problem.

(d) The fourth phase of the creative process is the period of insight. Out of the distressing incubation period the hints for solution come like a flash. The flashing hint for success is the insight which is accompanied by exhilaration, glow and elation as the person involved in the process is confident of his activity at the solution without much tension.

(e) Next phase of the creative process is the phase of construction. From the promptings received through the insight in the earlier stage the person at work in the creative process reaches the solution of the problem or meets the need faced in the first phase or produces the thing. This becomes possible through the realisation, elaboration and communication of the insight that has been experienced.

(f) The last and the final phase of the creative process is the phase or period of verification. The things, objects, devices, or ideas produced in the preceding stage is subjected to evaluation whether the product is able to serve the purpose or fulfil the need experienced and whether it is economical and worthwhile to adopt the device or follow the idea which was just discovered or developed in the earlier phase.

Whenever the last phase of verification is not done or made instantaneously there is always the risk that the creation or the product may be challenged and nullified to make room to a new one. Thus Newton's theory of light was replaced by another theory.

Almost all these six phases are noticed in the creative process leading to a successful creation may be a musical improvisation or Einstein's theory of Relativity.

Actually the creative process is a complex set of cognitive and motivational processes involving perceiving, remembering, thinking, imagining, deciding, etc. Guildford studied creativity from psychological perspective and attempted to conceptualize the intellectual processes involved in it. According to him, associated fluency, ideational fluency, originality, adaptive flexibility, spontaneous flexibility, dedication and sensitivity to problems are the criteria in a creative process. In a creative process there are the periods of enhancement and inhibition of creativity encouraging or depressing the creator.

4. The Creative Product

Any thing that is experienced or made by man, for example, an idea, a performance, a work of art, a scientific theory, may be called in general a creative product. But in a strict sense, a portion of those products which meets at least to some degree certain specified requirements or criteria will qualify as creative products.

The criteria or specific requirements in content of which a product is judged as creative are *novelty* or *originality, adaptiveness, elegance* and *transcendence*.

(a) The first requirement of a creative product is its novelty or originality. But that is not sufficient, because it faces the question as to what extent it is novel or original, i.e., much of young child's experiences and many of his ideas will be new to him and in that sense creative to him; but these experiences and ideas are ones that practically every child encounters in course of his growing up. They are not creative products of the society in which the child lives.

Thus the creativeness of a product, when judged in terms of its novelty, originality or statistical infrequencies is always relative to a given population or products. The most creative products are those that are novel or original in the experience of an entire civilization or of all mankind. May it be Raphael's work or Gallileo's discovery of earth's movement round the sun.

(b) Mere novelty or originality of a product is, however, not sufficient to justify its designation as creative. There is a second requirement that it must be adaptive to the reality. It must work to solve a problem, serve a purpose, fit the requirements of a given situation and accomplish some recognisable goal. Unless it is adaptable in reality a product may not be regarded as creative product in spite of its originality. For this reason the discovery of the process of making artificial diamond from coal failed to win the reputation of a *creative product.* There is also the need on the part of an artistic creation to be adoptable to reality, otherwise it will fail to win the reputation it deserves. Artistic creation, no less than a scientific creation, involves the solving of a problem, e.g., in painting we find a more appropriate expression of one's own experience indiscovering to convey more adequately a particular mood or theme, etc.

(c) The third requirement is that a creative product must meet the criterion of elegance, i.e., it is beautiful or at least aesthetically pleasing.

(d) The fourth criterion of a truly creative product is that it creates new conditions for human experience and existence. In order to do this it must transcend or transform the generally accepted experience of man by introducing new principle that defy tradition and radically change man's view of things. Examples of creative products have in their time transcended and transformed the then existing constraints of reality. For example, invention of railway and automobile engines and that of aeroplane have removed or transformed the constraints of conveyance. Similarly inventions of much improved devices in surgery removed or transformed the constraints of sickness.

(e) The fifth requirement of a creative product is that the insightful solution that underlies the product should be realised, evaluated, elaborated and developed to the full. It must be communicated and communicable to others and thereby it becomes usable when these aspects in the society of the products are visualized. In other words, the characteristics of a creative product should be such that it can be produced in numbers from the prototype and these should be usable in meeting demands.

Lastly, creative products are manifestation of creative activity. In other words, there are tangible expressions or resultants of creative activity.

In each field of creative enterprises there are several dimensions peculiar to the particular product. These are to be subjected to the above requirements or criteria, namely, originality, adaptiveness, elegance, transcendence and usability to make or stamp these as creative products.

Creativity and Education

So far we have made an anatomical dissection of creativity that embodies in itself the process of harmonizing. Creativity produced highest models of human achievement and awarded eternal distinction to man which cannot perish with time. It is a spontaneous unrepeatable and sometimes unpredictable quality that transcends simple mechanism such as computer. A set of pertinent question comes to mind. Is creativity related to education in any way? Why do we need creativity? What are the implications of creativity in education?

Answers to these questions demand a clarification. In reality it is not a process of certification, though many people think it in such terms. Education is necessarily a man-making process by which he is transformed into the desired man needed for the society. It is a process of human resource development. This development becomes effective through acquisition and application of necessary knowledge, skill and attitude. If education is thought in such terms, there is hardly any creative person who is not educated. A dive into the life and works of great creators reveals that they acquired necessary knowledge and skill in their own fields and many other related fields. Though creativity is a latest human quality, it is encouraged, improved and developed to distinction by education. There may be one Beethoven out of a group of people having some education. Education is a must like the manure and water for the flowering plant. Otherwise buds will wither and drop and creative ability will rest and perish.

We need education for creation and fulfilment of life. We need creativity in education to extend and transcend beyond the routine work of life, to enjoy bliss and achieve distinction. It is creativity in education which turns the toil of living into the joy of life. The journey in education is a journey without end, and creativity is the unceasing source of inspiration and joy in that journey; it is the seed of life for the length of living and leaving.

The relationship between creativity and education is, therefore, close. The growth of creativity in an individual depends upon the nature and character of the creative situation. But people differ in their responses to the same situation and conditions and as such it is difficult to prescribe a particular set of conditions and situations in education for inculcation of creativity among the learners. The following conditions and situations were generally found to be congenial for the growth of creativity among children in the school system:

1. A tendency to stress freedom and autonomy of the child.
2. Substitution of self-discipline or discipline inspected from outside.
3. An openness to all ideas and a judgement in choosing out of them.
4. The adoption of a more playful attitude to study.
5. Engagement in imaginative play and inculcation of appropriate imagery.
6. Initiation to search for common principles in terms of which quite different domains of knowledge can be related.
7. Nurture of a feeling for analogies, similies and metaphors not only in learning materials but also in life situations.

11

OUR STANDARD OF EDUCATION

There is an increasing skepticism on the educational standards in post-independence period of India. In a democracy, standards cannot be considered apart from the dominant values of a society. The aspirations and goals of a country and a nation should find expression through its educational system. Sociologically, standards may be viewed in several perspectives. They may seem to reflect the dominant cultural values of society. In this connection some pertinent questions may be raised as follows: Is a present-day graduate better or worse than his counterpart two or three decades ago? Has the concept of the educated undergone some drastic changes during the past few years? Questions such as these obsess the minds of all thinking persons.

On a critical analysis it would appear that a lot of confusion still prevails on the concept of standard. What is educational standard? Kripal of the Ministry of Education, while attempting to define standard, raises a pertinent question: "Do we judge the 'standard' by performance in public examination, or do we judge them by their physical fitness, or by their conduct and character"? There is yet another way of looking at the question. One would possibly enquire in this connection, whether

(a) there is any national standard, or

(b) there is any international standard fixed up. If so, how do the present standards compare?

The following steps are involved in the treatment of the particular issue:

1. A comprehensive definition of education should be evolved.
2. The objectives of education should be formulated with reference to the values.

3. The basal factors should be determined and a set of criteria fixed up for the sake of evaluation.

Let us take one by one the various dimensions of the problem for a thorough discussion.

Definiton of Education

No other definition of education is more comprehensive than Dewey's. According to him, education is life itself and as such should embrace all the facets or values of life and society. This view is rather too wide and extensive. The result is an attempt to reach a practical definition within a limited framework. The development of the inner potentialities, 'the manifestation of the perfection already in man' has been accepted as a tentative definition of education. Swami Vivekananda has emphasized the need for 'manifestation of the perfection already in man'.

While Swamiji has emphasised the need for self-manifestation, our monastic ideal was geared to self-realization. Tagore expressed the need for self-expression and development of heart along with the development of head and hand. It is, however, extremely difficult to find out the weightages of the different values attached.

The concept of educational standards thus needs clarification. It is felt that the problem is multi-dimensional. Various aspects of the educational standard point out the presence of a frame of reference for the purpose of comparison or evaluation. Now the question arises as to what would comprise the standard.

(a) a definite level of excellence or attainment in certain subject areas;

(b) a norm in performance, in practical or theoretical fields;

(c) a standard of development in certain skills, interests and habits;

(d) a standard behaviour including attitude;

(e) a level of cognitive ability including critical thinking; and

(f) a level of affective development.

Standard is not the same as norm or the criteria. A standard is based on what is good and desirable with reference to certain ends which determine them.

It is felt that no single criterion can satisfy the needs of our society and life. There are some relative values and a few absolute values in life which should be kept in view, while evaluating educational standard.

Need for a Scientific Enquiry

There is a good deal of controversy over the concept of a general standard which implies the process of comparison of educational performance and behavioural pattern displayed by the students at various levels.

What should form the criteria? No attempt has yet been made to develop a tool or an index of educational standards. For lack of such common criteria, educational experts have emphasised one or more of such criteria as examination results and job performances, skills in performances, skills in expression, social competence, etc.

A number of questions arise in this connection:

1. Is it a general term which could be used in connection with all subjects?
2. Could we measure educational sandards in terms of our expectations?
3. Should there be a majority rule determining whether something is a standard?

There is a good deal of vagueness surrounding the term 'educational standard'. It basically implies the process of comparison of educational performance of students at a particular stage or level with some absolute or relative criteria.

The word 'standard', according to dictionary, means anything taken as a basis of comparison or model and originates from the German word 'estandart'. Dictionary of Education explains the word in the following statements:

1. a goal or level of education expressed either numerically as a statistical average, or philosophically as an ideal of excellence.
2. any criterion by which things are judged.

Thus, a standard to be a comparable criterion or norm, has to be relative and not absolute, tangible and not abstract, objective and not biased, clear and not vague.

The notion of general standards should, therefore, be discarded in all scientific discussions. The specific standards are objectively comparable and measurable while the general standards are not comparable for lack of any absolute criteria. Standards derive their value from the value of something else.

Components of Index

Having clarified the meaning of educational standards, it is now possible to suggest some procedure for calculating an index for the rise of standards in education. There will be three major issues to be considered for determining the standard:

(a) fixing a base line for comparison

(b) fixing terms of reference or determinants and

(c) determining basal factors.

It is, however, important that any comparison demands some base line in respect of time or space or any other variable. If we take two distinct periods for comparison, viz., pre and post-independence periods in the history of education in India, we may possibly compare the standards in spite of a number of external variables the interaction between which are not known. It is a fact that the same set of circumstances cannot persist owing to the dynamic social forces, yet the standards are comparable in terms of basal products.

Quite a reasonable demand for qualitative fundamentals for objective assessment may be placed for attacking this problem. For example, instead of going for examination results, we may think of standard in terms of fundamental potetialities, e.g., critical thinking, creativity, social sensitivity, and some of the basic qualities of head and heart. It is felt that the evaluation of the standard is rendered feasible, if the number of variables for assessment can be controlled.

Collection of Data

If we assume that our educational standards are falling, we should have the relevant data collected by means of suitable techniques at our disposal. The nature of data should, of course, have a reference to the educational objectives. If our purpose is to compare the academic achievements, techniques would be evolved accordingly. But how could we avail of the achievement means or averages of a particular section of population? Results are hardly dependable for such purpose, because of the changing policy of the educational authorities from time to time. Moreover, the percentage of passes of any class obtained by students are not clearly indicative of the standards.

If such are the problems in case of comparing academic achievement, there would be more complicated problems on the way to comparison of standards with reference to qualities of heart and hand. The techniques of collecting the data should vary according to situation and should consist of ratings, opinions, and questionnaire on the one hand and objective tests, on the other.

In the circumstances, no scientific enquiry has been conducted as yet to offer any conclusive evidence of the falling or rising standard. In a symposium organized by the Centre of Advanced Studies in Education, Baroda, it has been observed that standards very at different levels and there can hardly be any convincing results obtained except from the stray observations forwarded by the speakers belonging to various disciplines.

Some Concluding Observations

If we consider educational standards at various levels, our opinions would vary. Let us take the question stage by stage:

1 *At the pre-primary Level.* This is a stage at which education was mainly entrusted with parents and there was hardly any formal education for the children at this stage. During recent years, learning situations at this level have improved and greater amenities are provided, particularly in towns and cities. Yet it is difficult to say whether educational standard has improved or not, because here also the issue has to to be determined with reference to the values attached to the goals to be reached. If the aesthetic value is given preference to others, the standard appears to have gone up, as the children today are made more sensitive and alert to the environment by greater stimulations. So far as the academic standard is concerned, it is at least clear that attempts are now being made to stimulate the child's experiences in a more systematic manner. But the result is yet to be evaluated.

2. *At the Primary Level.* The first thing in collecting evidences regarding standards at the elementary stage, should be to select such schools where the student population can be fairly compared with that of the schools during the pre-independence period.

The comparison of the standards at the two periods is not an easy task and as such we could take into account some symptoms for locating the standard.

3. *School Curricula.* In the past, the course was stereotyped and objectives narrow. But now, with elementary education being conceived as the minimum essential education of the citizens of democratic India, the school curricula have grown both in dimension and in content. But one wonders whether things have improved in other directions as well. If we judge standards by the dimension of the

curriculum, one would be tempted to jump to the conclusion that educational standards at the primary level are going up. But is it based on scientific analysis of factual data?

If we take the academic value as the determining factor, we would be at a loss to come to a definite conclusion. Where is the evidence that academically the children at the primary level today are better or worse than before? As regards the development of fundamental potentials, it is rather very uncertain as to whether the width of the curriculum has contributed to the promotion of the standard. Observations, however, point out that the picture is not encouraging and the children today are gaining more alertness and sensitivity at the cost of thoroughness.

The reasons are not far to seek. The values in education are at conflict here as well. There are values ethical, moral, social and economic, besides academic. As we are still confused as to which value should receive prominence or priority, our educational programmes are failing to follow any particular direction.

4. *Standard at the Secondary Level.* Sri Prem Kripal has rightly pointed out that there is little clarity in the minds of people, and quite a number of observers think in terms of examination results, particularly in subjects like English. If we take percentage of pass as an index of standard, we fail to reach any definite conclusion. A study made by the Directorate of Extension Programmes in Secondary Education reveals that the results of most Boards of Secondary Education varied only slightly from year to year. It will thus appear that examination results do not furnish any reliable evidence of the standard in secondary schools. It has also been observed that failures in matriculation examination from the earliest years were largely due to poor results in English. So far as the other criteria are concerned one might think that pupils at the secondary level today are better informed of the outside world, more politically conscious and alert to environment.

Before enumerating some of the specific areas of deterioration, it would be worth while to say that there are some fundamental or basic aspects of educational standards which can hardly be ignored. For instance, an educated person must have developed in him

(1) an attitude of 'live and let live';

(2) respect for others' views and tolerance;

(3) a conviction that 'all human being are equal' in addition to

(a) general knowledge;

(b) proficiency in the application of knowledge;

(c) critical thinking;

and other personality qualities. Now this is again the question of values which would determine the issue. The question will remain unanswered until the criterion in terms of value is fixed up. This will remain a controversy as will be evident from few observations. Sardar Panikar, formerly Vice-Chancellor of the University of Mysore, observed that the standard of education in the country had not fallen as alleged by some people, but had gone up, while Sri Prem Kripal has indirectly supported the hypothesis that our educational standards are falling at certain levels in certain respects. So far as standards at university level are concerned, the same controversy would persist. The problems may vary in dimensions, but fundamentally most of them are alike.

There are various dimensions of educational standard. The continuous change in the composition of various factors of education stands on the way to any sound comparison. Curriculum, teachers, methodology, evaluation, etc., are changing in a dynamic set-up. In spite of the fact that all the changes are affected for the sake of betterment of standards, there is a growing dissatisfaction with the present educational standard. It may be that this feeling is partly due to emotional attachment with the impression 'when we were young'. But is it the only reason?

There may be another possibility that the modern age has highest demands on our education with the expanding frontiers of knowledge. In that case we will have to survey our various needs and evaluate the educational standard with reference to each of the needs forming the criteria.

This seems to be a better proposition. Instead of trying to compare standards at two different periods, it would be perhaps more worthwhile to investigate into our present emerging needs as well as outstanding values in life, and plan our educational programme to meet those adequately. It would be a wild goose chase, if we fail to control the variables of background before comparing on an objective basis. Whether our educational standards are falling or not, would thus remain a subjective and debatable question, unless adequate data could be collected and interpreted with scientific precision. There is, of course, a general consensus that we are gaining more and more in range and less and less in depth.

There is a strong feeling that students today are more informed and less thorough, more sensitive but less critical, mere distracted and less concentrating and persistent.

So far as the values of life are concerned, the picture appears to be blurred by so many images. It appears that the present student population tends to be less introspective with varied interests, more pragmatic and confused and less interested in knowledge for the sake of knowledge. These are, however, some of the general impressions formed by a particular group of thinkers.

It is indeed a gratifying phenomenon that 'old order changes yielding place to new', but it reflects a fluctuating tendency. When one sits to examine that oft-quoted statement beginning with 'old is gold' on the one hand, and 'new is noble', on the other extreme, it leads us nowhere, if we merely continue to relish the past glory and condemn the new change. Similarly, it is equally stagnating if we close our eyes to the past and fail to evaluate the change with reference to the emerging values of life. The values of life are unfortunately at cross-roads as it is essential to determine the values in order of priority before undertaking any other exploration of this nature.

12

PEACE AND EDUCATION

Peace is the living principle of nature as well as mankind. It is all about the living organisms we care for. If we look at the nature we see all distortions and calamities ultimately end and tranquillity comes back. In our human life as well, we see that peace is inherent in us. It is affected by some outward disturbances, ignorance of some human beings and misunderstandings among a few individuals. Peace is a discipline, it should be practised in the life of every human being. Education is there to help mankind to find out what we are for in this world. It is harmony and peace. According to Dean Gooderham Acheson, "Peace is positive, and it has to be waged with all our thought, energy and courage". Children need education for peace to develop right attitude of life. To quote Albert Einstein, "Peace cannot be kept by force. It can only be achieved by understanding. It is essential that the student acquires an understanding of and a lively feeling for values. He must acquire a vivid sense of the beautiful and of the normally good. The school should always have as its aim that the young man learns it as a harmonious personality". Our learned teacher, Dr. S. Radhakrishnan states that "Education for peace should encourage the exercise of these qualities—adventure in the world of spirit, the tradition of tolerance, the instinct of live and let live, these are deeply ingrained in us. Men are born for love and friendship and not hatred and war.... It is the task of education, to create in us a love for the new world of peace and fellowship". In this reference we should mention the name of R.P. Masani who suggests that the teachers can use materials for fostering world loyalties, a sense of moral values, the dignity and freedom of the human spirit. Teacher education, as Mohammad Sherif Khan states, is "teachers' training plus the theoretical framework and philosophical foundation in a field of education". To quote Medougall, "Teachers make their effect more by what they are than what they do" Pandit Jawaharlal Nehru says,

"Peace cannot suddenly be deserved from the heavens. It can only come when the root cause of trouble are removed" We know, avarice, ambition, envy, anger and pride are five great enemies to peace that inhabits with us.

Objectives Necessary for Education of Peace

1. The teacher should develop in students appreciation of importance of co-operative living, atmosphere of social confidence, hope and securities.
2. The teacher should help students to develop an understanding and skills for corporate feeling and feeling of social purpose, to guard against separatist tendencies of language, religion and province.
3. The teacher should help pupils to develop insight into the functioning of group activities and social services for the welfare of the community wherein they live.
4. The teacher should help students to develop awareness of use of Panchasila in educational set-ups.

PLAN OF PROPOSAL FOR PEACE-EDUCATION

I. Instruction materials through subjects taught in school, need to be rightly selected, organized and presented following certain basic principles such as:

(a) These should be selected in accordance with the purpose of education for peace and harmony.

(b) Care should be taken that children get their first picture of the past heritage and culture from historical tales and prejudices inculcated at their early ages.

(c) Social science should have to be supplemented by social philosophy and social ethics for peace.

(d) The meaning of secularism should be explained on proper perspective, i.e., "Secularism requires us not merely to tolerate, but to understand and love other religions."

(e) Science education should be based on the realization that nuclear weapons should be turned into the service of peace and human welfare.

II. Group discussions and Debates on Peace their values in Life. Certain activity-oriented plans should be organized such as:

(a) Necessity for developing habits of exchanging opinions and thoughts among age-mates of various provinces, countries and nations in favour of peace and harmony.

(b) Guidance should be given to participants to develop an attitude to speak and listen easily, sympathetically and without fear.

(c) Critical analyses should be made among pupils about damages of a narrow nationalism. Encouragement should be made for realising the importance of pen-friendship.

(d) The teacher should endow pupils with a purposive-enfranchisement of the mind, freedom from prejudices, and fanaticism, to develop right outlook for harmony and peace.

III. Audio-visual aids in favour of Peace and Harmony should be provided to students to develop better understanding of national and international cultures, historical facts and world's progress for which certain specific measures need to be adopted by teachers such as:

(a) Books and films for children and adolescents should be carefully prepared, selected and scrutinized before giving to their pupils for developing awareness of peace.

(b) Care should be taken that there must be no wrong informations about other nations or other cultures and countries or misdirective ideas against peace.

(c) Radio and television programmes should be selected so that children may realize the value of peace and harmony. Peace programmes must have scope for vitality, wide imagination and perpetual vigilance; need of fellowship, common ideals and definite purpose of human peace.

IV. Daily prayer that portrays about peace and integration is essential for school children.

Whatever may be, Language of prayer, the contents should convey "Meet together, talk together. May your minds comprehend alike. Common be your action and achievement. Common be your thoughts and intentions. Common be the wishes of your hearts, so there may be thorough Union among you."

— S. Radhakrishnan

V. Field experiences in some selected areas should be provided to pupils for better understanding of peace as follows:

(a) Interest-groups should be organized by students, e.g., clubs and societies to discuss freely on Peace.

(b) Publication of magazines should be arranged on peace movements in our country and abroad.

(c) Community education project should be organized to motivate peace approaches.

(d) Inter-school and inter-college unions should be organized to write dramas on peace and to stage such dramas co-operatively among students of various countries.

(e) Camp-living should be provided to lead corporate life.

(f) Parent-teacher meetings should be frequently organized to discuss on harms of war movements, terrorism and their horrors to provide healthy care for children, motivate them towards peace and harmony.

VI. Seminars and workshops on Peace and Harmony should be arranged so that children, under the guidance of their teachers, may have scope for doing following activities right from their school days:

(a) Extempore lectures on peace and its effect on human progress.

(b) Mini literature on peace programme may be prepared and published by students as classroom projects.

(c) Exhibition of paintings on the value of peace and horror of war may be arranged by pupils by themselves.

(d) Some projects on Peace and Harmony, may be organized by adolescent pupils under the supervision of teachers.

VII. Some innovative researches on peace and harmony may be encouraged among the high school students.

In conclusion, let me state that our teacher-education programme should pay more emphasis on developing right attitude among teacher-trainees. They should realize what Dr. Radhakrishnan means: "All systems of education aim at the education of the whole man. The main line of work in the teacher-education system, I hope, should be more dynamic and peace-oriented."

THE MOST NEEDED EDUCATION OF THE DAY

The first task of an educator or any enlightened citizen of India is to provide scope for developing the excellences that each child has. These excellences are mainly innate in the child. They are only to be lighted up by giving him appropriate environment. In the words of Swami Vivekananda, "Education is the manifestation of the perfection already in man". We have been mishandling our children and do not provide proper environment for the growth. We lack in our sincerity.

Even after 35 years that the Constitution of independent India came into force 66 per cent of the people of India are literally illiterate. The democracy of our country has thus remained a misnomer. The politicians are exploiting the illiterate mass to gain their vested interest, thereby turning the franchise of the people to a mockery. They are banking upon the illiteracy and ignorance of the mass to fulfil their political ends. Thomas Jefferson, one of the founders of the U.S.A., remarked, "If a nation expects to be ignorant and free, it expects what never was and never will be".

Peace is a boon of affluent democracy. For this we need educational institutions which aim at culturing excellences among the people. Every child has some excellences. They are to be cultivated and cultured by the society for meeting the real educational needs of the country. We cannot be a prototype of China or Russia or U.S.A. We can be only Indian with Indian excellences cultured, thereby turning us out to be a prominent up-to-date nation of the world. It does not mean that we shall not imbibe the good cultures of the foreign lands. The power of imbibing of good cultures is a great art. Excellences, though mainly innate, are also to be gathered from inside the country as well from outside the country. Thus only we can have education in its true sense.

National or international peace can come only through citizenship education. This education is much more than acquiring skill. A skilled person may be an engineer, a technician or even a thief or a murderer. But an educated person has the regional, national and international understanding, through which he brings social and super-social goods. He can criticise all problems sanely and squarely, and act accordingly.

Self-concept is the basis for assimilation of education. Self-culture and self-education provide self-enlightenment and can lead to the attainment of ultimate realisation of self. This only leads to proper understanding of others. This can be had only through moral education in its real sense. Man and man are brothers when they are educated, even though their views may differ; but they are enemies, when uneducated, since they cannot stand the difference of views of others. Thus peace of mind is disturbed. Peace can emanate only from the right type of education. The League of Nations or the United Nations Organization may be the first step for establishing the peace of the world. But the nations are sure to break away, if they are not very

F1-82

willing partners. The veto-right of the big powers hampers peaceful solution of international problems. Hence this should be abolished from the UNO.

Atomic energy, electronic discoveries, medical advances and space explorations are boons to human knowledge and achievements. If these are utilised for human development and peace, they can do a lot of good to the people of the world. They can control the population explosion giving an eugenic advancement, better living conditions and international understanding.

The cultural activities of Santiniketan and the culture radiated by our great poet, educator and philanthropist Rabindra Nath Tagore or by the great dancers and musicians like Udai Sankar, Rabi Sankar, Timir Baran and Bare Gulam Ali and the artists like Nandalal Bose and sculptors like Ramkinkar Bej will be leading to a great extent to the establishment of harmony and international peace of the world.

The proposed National Cultural Centre or "Centre of National Integration" at Santiniketan is a step forward toward the attainment of national and international understanding by the people of India. According to Sri Janajit Roy's views expressed in his article "Making Tagore's Dream Come True" published in the magazine of the Telegraph dated 15 September, 1985, the centre will conduct studies on the theme of synthesis of India's spiritual, philosophical and ethical thought and the development of India's art, architecture, music, dance and drama to illustrate the cultural unity of India. We heartily welcome the establishment of this centre.

REFERENCES

1. Collected Lectures of Dr. S. Radhakrishnan, *Education for World Understanding.*
2. Shrimali K. L., *Human Relations in Teacher Education.*
3. Mohammad Sharif Khan, *Teacher Education in India and Abroad.*
4. P. Gurrey, *Education and the Training of Teachers.*